Alesha

Alesha

Her Story – The Unauthorized Biography

Anna Tripp

MICHAEL O'MARA BOOKS

First published in Great Britain in 2009 by
Michael O'Mara Books Limited
9 Lion Yard
Tremadoc Road
London SW4 7NQ

Copyright © Michael O'Mara Books Limited 2009

A CIP catalogue record for this book is available from the British Library.

Papers used by Michael O'Mara Books Limited are natural, recyclable products
made from wood grown in sustainable forests. The manufacturing processes
conform to the environmental regulations of the country of origin.

Hardback ISBN: 978-1-84317-443-1
Trade paperback ISBN: 978-1-84317-449-3

1 3 5 7 9 10 8 6 4 2

www.mombooks.com

Cover design by Zoe Quayle
Designed and typeset by K. DESIGN, Winscombe, Somerset
Plate section designed by Ana Bjezancevic
Printed in the UK by CPI William Clowes Beccles NR34 7TL

Contents

To my own little diva, with love.

Acknowledgements

I'd like to thank my fantastic editor Louise Dixon and everyone at Michael O'Mara Books for their encouragement and help, especially Anna Marx, Judy Parkinson, Zoe Quayle and Ana Bjezancevic, and Kay Hayden for her fantastic typesetting skills.

The following newspapers, magazines and websites have been invaluable: *The Times*, *The Daily Telegraph*, *The Guardian*, *The Observer*, Press Association, *The Sun*, *The Mirror*, *The News of the World*, *The People*, *The Daily Star*, *The Daily Express*, *The Sunday Express*, *The Sunday Mirror*, *The Sunday Mail*, *Liverpool Echo*, *Birmingham Mail*, *Birmingham Post*, *South Wales Echo*, *Cosmopolitan* and *Designer* magazine, www.ilikemusic.com, www.gm.tv, www.bbc.co.uk/strictlycomedancing and www.youtube.com.

Finally, a huge thanks goes to my children and my wonderful husband for their patience and for putting up with 'the lost summer ...'

Picture Credits

Page 9   Jane Mingay/PA Archive/Press Association Images
(*top*); Tony Kyriacou/Rex Features (*bottom left*);
Fred Duval/FilmMagic/Getty Images (*bottom right*)

Page 10 © Jeff Spicer/Alpha

Page 11 Dominic Lipinski/PA Archive/Press Association
Images (*top*); Richard Kendal/Retna Pictures (*bottom left*); Brian Rasic/Rex Features (*bottom right*)

Page 12 © Edward Lloyd/Alpha (*top left*); Chris Jepson/
FAMOUS (*top right*); Jo Hale/Getty Images (*bottom*)

Page 13 © Alpha (*top*); Tom Shaw/Getty Images (*bottom left*);
Brian O'Sullivan/EMPICS Entertainment/Press
Association Images (*bottom right*)

Page 14 Chris Jackson/Comic Relief via Getty Images
(*top left & right*); Jonathan Hordle/Rex Features
(*bottom*)

Page 15 Gareth Davies/Getty Images (*top left*); Yui Mok/
PA Wire/Press Association Images (*top right*);
Brian O'Sullivan/EMPICS Entertainment/Press
Association Images (*bottom*)

Page 16 © Gareth Gay/Alpha

Also with special thanks for their help to Warren Bacci of the
Top Hat Stage School, and Beverley Harris.

Introduction

From rasping rapper to belle of the ballroom, Alesha Dixon's transformation on *Strictly Come Dancing* in the autumn of 2007 had viewers enthralled. 'She does class and she does sexy,' raved Italian judge Bruno Tonioli. 'She does beauty and she does beast. What more do you want?' But while her lively Latin and elegant ballroom won the judges' approval, it was her bubbly nature, abundant energy and constant cackling laugh that lifted her from underground garage star to the darling of the nation.

The smile, as the audience knew only too well, hid a world of pain and heartbreak.

Just one year earlier, Alesha's life had come crashing down around her. After enjoying top ten hits with girl band Mis-Teeq, she had embarked on a solo career and was on the verge of releasing an album when her label unexpectedly ditched her. Just two weeks later the tabloids reported that her husband of just over a year, MC Harvey, was having an affair with Javine Hylton, his co-star in the West End musical *Daddy Cool*.

Devastated, it took months for Alesha to pick herself up, but signing up for *Strictly* proved the best move of her life. 'Dancing saved me,' she said, and the audience tuned in every week in their millions to watch the sassy singer fight back.

The same fighting spirit had already brought her from a difficult childhood in a poverty-stricken area, where she was bullied because of the colour of her skin, to finding chart success with a band dubbed 'Britain's answer to Destiny's Child'.

It took her from the lows of rejection to the dizzy heights of Kilimanjaro, climbing alongside some of the UK's biggest celebrities to raise money for Comic Relief. And it saw her rebuild her solo career with two top ten hits and a platinum album. With her latest challenge taking her from contestant to judge on the show that turned her life around, Alesha is once more at the top of her game.

This books charts the highs and lows of the inspirational celebrity who is living proof that when you hit rock bottom, the only way is up.

CHAPTER ONE

Can I Begin?

You would be forgiven for assuming that, as a streetwise, sassy singer and rapper, once married to a member of the So Solid Crew, Alesha Dixon grew up in the rougher parts of south London. In fact she was born and bred in Welwyn Garden City, a new town nestling in the rural surroundings of Hertfordshire.

'There are lots of woods and horses. We have a Shredded Wheat factory and to be honest, it's very quiet,' Alesha told *FHM* magazine. 'You rarely hear a police siren or an ambulance. Occasionally there are some teenagers fighting on a Saturday night, but that's it.'

Welwyn Garden City is famous as the birthplace of Shredded Wheat and Shreddies, and former residents of the town include Nick Faldo, BBC Director-General Mark Thompson and fellow *Strictly Come Dancing* contestant Lisa Snowdon. Built in 1919, as a housing project designed by social reformer Ebenezer Howard to improve the quality of life of workers and to give them 'fresh air, sunlight, breathing space and playing room', the town was intended to reflect the 'gifts of nature', so that 'life became an abiding joy and delight'.

Whether or not life was an abiding joy and delight for her penniless mum, Alesha, who later moved back to the town, remembers taking advantage of the wide-open spaces around it to spend long summer days outside. 'All we could see at the end of our road was fields. In the summer we used to have these long, idyllic days that never seemed to end,' she said. 'We would always escape to the river nearby. I used to have a dog, Shep, who would chase behind — and if it was a sunny day, my mum wouldn't see me till 10pm.'

Born on 7 October 1978, Alesha Anjanette Dixon was the second of three children who mum Beverley had by different partners. Her father, Jamaican electrician Melvin Dixon, left when Alesha was just four years old. After the split, Beverley struggled to make ends meet and some sacrifices had to be made to put food on the table. For Alesha, who already showed signs of the twinkle toes that won her the *Strictly Come Dancing* trophy some years later, that meant her beloved ballet and tap classes had to stop. Instead she put her skills to use in the school playground.

'We made up dances in the school playground and performed them in school assembly — it's what we lived for.

'The only time I would get to dance was at school, doing the choreography for plays. It's not a sob story. It's just the reality of where I come from and how it was.'

The ever-optimistic Alesha, however, looks on her upbringing as a lesson in life. 'Everybody has things they go through that aren't perfect, that's what shapes us,' she told *The Sun*. 'I come from a single-parent family. How many people come from single-parent families, where the mum can't afford to buy them nice things or send them to dance classes? It's reality.

'I'd rather have a lovely mum who supports me than go to stage school. I was always aware we didn't have much, but I knew I still had everything. I would never have put my mum under so much pressure by asking to go to dance classes — so I made up routines on the playground and teamed up with friends for a local competition. But still, I would look at other countries and think, "Oh my God, I have electricity, a loving mum and dad and clothes on my back," I wasn't starving.'

Rather than bringing her down, her lack of advantage in life made the young Alesha into a natural born fighter, strong-minded and resolute. If something looked difficult to accomplish, she carried on trying until she achieved her goal.

'I've always been very determined, from when I was very young,' she has said.

'My mum says that I was the kind of child that, if I couldn't tie my shoelaces and she offered to help, I'd say, "No, I'll do it." Even though I was aware that things weren't perfect, I always chose to look at what I did have. I didn't have nice clothes, didn't have a mobile phone and couldn't afford to go to dance classes. But what we did have was a lot of love. My mum's an artist and we were very creative with the things we did; very imaginative. 'They say, don't they, that if you can visualize yourself doing something, you can make it happen. I felt that, even from a very young age. I always imagined myself doing exactly what I'm doing now – I saw myself on stage and travelling the world.'

With practice and determination Alesha and her crew became quite skilful at their dance routines and even attracted some promising attention. 'We got quite good and we got entered into a national dance competition, Super Dance,' she recalled. 'We were the only group of people at the competition that were not from a proper dance group and we even made our own costumes.'

In another interview she revealed that her impoverished childhood has made her determined to find happiness, but not at the cost of others. 'Growing up, we didn't have a telephone, mum didn't drive a car and all my mates would have new clothes while I wore the same pair of jeans for two weeks,' she told *Cosmopolitan* magazine. 'I was rich in many other ways. My ambition in life isn't to make money; it's to be happy and be a good person, and do things that stimulate me … I like to drive a nice car, live in a nice house and buy nice clothes, but they don't make me who I am.'

Sadly for Alesha, not every member of her family was able to put such a positive spin on life at home. As the dancing diva swept her way to victory on *Strictly* in 2007 the only cloud on the horizon was a warts-and-all account of their childhood, sold to a tabloid by Alesha's older brother Mark. According to his heavily disputed version of events, Beverley's relationships with men were often violent, and on one occasion the two horrified children watched her lover beat her.

'Around the time our brother John was born, and Alesha was just ten, there was an altercation between Mum and her boyfriend,' Mark told the *News of the World*. 'The guy started to attack her so she legged it out of the house. I'll never forget seeing her running down the street, him leaping on her and breaking her ribs with the force of his body weight. We were watching from the window and Alesha and I were screaming at him to get off our mum. That time she ended up going to hospital, but the guy didn't leave and the violence just continued.

'We'd hear fighting downstairs after we'd gone to bed and next morning there'd always be a new bruise or swollen eye which Mum would lie about, saying she'd fallen or something. We knew this man was beating her up but there was nothing we could do. Instead, me and Alesha would huddle together and secretly slag him off behind his back. It was our way of fighting him.

'Eventually Mum split with the guy and that was our chance to tell him what we really thought of him. Alesha didn't hold back and the rows got really heated. The guy never got physical but he was threatening and the police got involved. He was told never to come around to the house again.'

During another relationship, the two children were forced to share their bedroom with their mother's new partner's two kids, according to Mark. 'This guy cut the room in half with a plasterboard partition,' he said. 'There we were all in single beds. It was a squished-up existence with no room to swing a cat.

'One night the other two kids were crying over something but Alesha and I had a fit of the giggles and couldn't stop laughing. Their dad got really angry and finally stormed upstairs to tan our backsides.'

Mark went on to accuse his mother of leaving the children starving because she had no money to buy food, a claim that Alesha vehemently refutes.

'The last thing I would ever want is people to think my mum is a bad mother — she's the most amazing mother anybody could ever wish for,' Alesha said at the time. 'I am fuming, because anyone who could accuse anybody of starving their children is just beyond ludicrous. Let's talk about Ethiopia — that's what real starvation is about.'

The singer is fiercely protective of her mother and they remain incredibly close, in spite of, or perhaps because of, the traumas they have been through as a family. As a result of the article, the usually affable Alesha cut ties with brother Mark.

'The reason I don't talk to Mark is because of the way he is so disrespectful to our mum,' she told *The Sun*. 'I cherish her. If anyone is rude about her or says a bad word about her they won't be a part of my life. Unfortunately, that's how I feel about my brother.'

She will admit, however, that her mother's lovers weren't always the nicest of guys. 'When I was a little girl I saw things I wish I hadn't,' she has said. 'One of the hardest things is seeing the person you love the most being hurt. But everything that has happened to me has shaped me and made me a strong person. My mum is wonderful and I would never want people thinking badly about her. I felt betrayed by Mark.'

Despite the betrayal, she wishes no ill on her big brother. 'I love my brother and wish nothing but good things for him,' she said.

Music and dance provided some escapism for Alesha during her childhood years. 'Madonna is a big idol. I loved her when I was a young girl and feel like I've been on a musical journey with her,' she revealed later. 'Even Pink Floyd, which my mum used to play in the house. It's great to be able to take all the influences and mix them together.'

In terms of role models, Alesha looked towards Lauryn Hill, Michael Jackson and, particularly, mixed-race star Neneh Cherry as proof that someone who shared her skin colour could be a star.

As a mixed-race child in a predominantly white area Alesha also had to contend with the spectre of racism throughout her school years. The fact that her brother was white only served to add fuel to the flames of bigotry in the small town. 'I can't pretend it wasn't confusing,' she told *The Times*. 'Having people at school ask me about my family and having to draw diagrams.

Being mixed race as well, you get asked why one of your brothers is white and another one is black. Tell that to some kids and it just doesn't compute.'

As she's got older she would admit that her large disparate family has become a positive in her life, providing her with a great deal of comfort. Her love for all her family means she has plenty of brothers, sisters, cousins, nieces and nephews around her. 'I've always got someone to turn to,' Alesha said in 2008. 'My oldest brother's got five children, so it's nice to be the favourite auntie – when I get to take them to things like the *High School Musical* premiere. But then I can't keep up with all their birthdays and I feel guilty.

'When I was younger, I didn't like it. My siblings are all over the place as my mum and dad split up when I was little – but now I appreciate it. I'm blessed.'

After the relative safety of her primary school, Alesha found the local comprehensive, Monk's Walk secondary, brought name calling and bullying although, according to brother Mark, she dealt with it stoically and never told a soul. After he discovered through the school grapevine that one racist pupil was calling Alesha names, Mark and some other lads gave the perpetrator a hiding and he was promptly expelled from school.

'When I first joined my school, some people called me racist names and I remember my brother actually having someone up by the neck outside the headmaster's office and dropping him on the floor,' recalls Alesha. 'That instinct and brotherly love was always there the moment anyone tried to do me harm.'

Alesha is philosophical about the name calling and believes the majority of the public is not racist. After suggestions in the newspapers that the *Strictly Come Dancing* audience had voted

Don Warrington and Heather Small out of the contest because of their skin colour, she spoke out in *The Sun* to defend the voters. 'If it was racist, how could I have won? I think it's a storm in a teacup. I actually think that's quite insulting to the British public. The truth is that the public vote when they like someone's personality as well as when they like their dancing. Some people have bigger fan bases than others, that's all.

'When I was a child I used to get called names, like "chocolate bar" or stupid things like that. But that was just ignorant kids. I haven't experienced it since and I would never use my skin colour as an excuse. If I don't win something or a song fails to get to number one, it's because I'm not good enough.'

While backing an anti-bullying campaign in 2006, she admitted that one group of girls made her life a misery. 'There was a gang of girls who used to intimidate me when I was about sixteen. We used to hang out in the same club but I was always scared they'd attack or abuse me,' she recalled. 'Bullying consumes your mind completely, which is why you need to say something to someone – because bullies thrive on fear and when you speak up you take away their power.'

At Monk's Walk school, Alesha was a bright pupil and fared well in most subjects, but her passion was sport. Gymnastics was a particular favourite, and as a teenager, she was so advanced that she turned to coaching others. She also adored drama and dance and put her excess energy into enjoying the activities she loved, saying she spend her childhood, 'singing, dancing, playing sports'.

'Going through school I actually wanted to be a sports teacher. I did a diploma in sports studies and coached gymnastics. I was very active and I've always loved anything that's physical.'

*

The split between her mother and father was an acrimonious one and, after Melvin left the family home, he entered a new relationship and went on to have three more children. Although Alesha remained close to her paternal grandmother, Clem, she saw very little of Melvin, who kept in contact with occasional visits during the year. At Christmas, Alesha found the tug of love left her with a difficult decision.

'My mum and dad don't really like each other, so when Christmas came along, that could be a bit stressful,' she said to *The Times*. 'It almost became a political thing, who you were going to spend Christmas with. My mother was cool about it. But my dad got a bit funny if I stayed over and it was time to go back. You would spend your whole life juggling.'

Even so, Alesha's brother Mark claimed that her relationship with her paternal family often provided his sister with a respite from life at home. 'She turned to Melvin and his family, particularly his mum, Clem, as an escape,' explained Mark in the *News of the World*. 'When life at home got too traumatic for her she'd go and stay with them in London. It's like she buried her head in the sand to pretend things weren't as bad as they seemed.'

The one event Alesha always attended with her father was the annual Notting Hill Carnival. Eager to educate her about her Caribbean roots, Melvin would pick his daughter up on the first day of the popular festival and take her to London, where she would try the Jamaican food from the stalls and hear music she never heard in Welwyn Garden City. Unlike her teen years, when she would attend with her girlfriends and attract unwanted attention from groups of guys, she always felt protected with Melvin and these days out had a huge influence on her musical tastes. 'All the dancehall records I saved up to buy – Shabba Ranks, Buju Banton – I heard them at Notting Hill.'

Her father and grandmother, both passionate cooks, also had a huge influence on Alesha's culinary tastes, and she loves West Indian cuisine. 'Being mixed race I'm lucky to have that contrast – having a white family and a black family and being able to appreciate each culture for what it is,' she told *The Observer*. 'Food is natural in Jamaica. You're driving along and you pick up a jelly coconut. In my uncle's garden they have an ackee tree. The last time I visited I sat with his wife picking ackee, cracking open the huge hard red shells and prising the yellow fruit off the black stone. Jamaican food is not instant. You can't just whip it up. We like to season the meat the night before, and cook it slowly. With oxtail you cook it for hours until it falls off the bone. When I'm working I go to takeaways, or my [Jamaican] nan's because she's always got something on the pot. She's the queen of cooking, I'm yet to find anyone who can beat her.'

While her father and grandmother stimulated her tastebuds, another member of the family, her Uncle Leroy, was responsible for Alesha's budding career as an MC. The scattergun style that brought her to the public's attention when Mis-Teeq exploded onto the pop scene had its roots in the parties she attended with him as a teenager. But, as a girl, she had to fight her way onto the mike.

'I was getting the guts to go up to people at parties and saying to them, "Can I have a go on the mike?" Nine times out of ten they'd say no because I'm female, but I would just hang around until they let me.'

Even her uncle didn't take her seriously at first, but she soon won the crowd over and said she enjoyed the fact that guys expected female MCs to fall flat on their faces because, 'it's a real laugh when you see them thinking, "S***, she can actually do this!"'

She freely admits that some of her lyrics from the early days were a little cringeworthy. Speaking to *The Daily Telegraph* she said, 'I was drawn in by the energy and power, the sense of controlling the crowd. There were no females doing it, so it was a novelty when I would get on the mike in my nice dress. 'I had this one lyric I would do: "You're nicer than the chicken and the rice and the gravy/You're so damn lovely, I'll be your wife and I'll have your babies." It was so cheesy, but it always got a good response, probably because of the dress, and that gave me the confidence to develop.'

While Alesha found her voice at the mike, an alternative ambition to become a PE teacher led her to apply for a place at Loughborough University, which she got. At the same time she found a street dance class in London and, supported by Beverley, who would give her daughter her last £10 for the train fare, she began to travel to Bond Street every Sunday. Two fateful meetings on the second Sunday meant Alesha never made it to her university course.

'There I was, eighteen years old, going up there on the train and I was really scared. And on the second Sunday I was approached in the dance class by a scout from a production company. And on the way back, someone else approached me on the train!' Both turned out to be genuine offers to help her in the world of showbusiness. An excited Alesha rushed home and told her mum, 'I think it might all be happening!' then she ditched the PE course and embarked on four years of struggling as a fledgling artist.

Dad Melvin had other plans for his talented daughter, however. He was sceptical about her chances of making it in the music industry and was keen to see her study to become an accountant or a barrister. Headstrong and determined, the teenager refused to give up. 'I'll never forget that conversation. He said, "Well, I understand that you love singing, but you have to look at the market, and there aren't many successful British black artists." I remember saying to him, "I can't make my decisions in life based on other people's successes and failures." I thank my dad, because he gave me the drive to say, "You know what? I'm going to prove we can sell."'

Alesha's upbringing, by her own admission, was less than perfect, but it has left the singer with a deep sense of family and loyalty, and a grounding in reality. As well as an unbreakable bond with her mum, she enjoys a very close relationship with both her grandmothers, who became celebrities in their own right as they supported her week after week when she appeared on *Strictly Come Dancing*.

Maureen, Beverley's mum, told the cameras 'It's been a sheer delight watching you dance. Good luck, sweetheart. I love you very much and I hope you win.' Whereas Clem, watching every week, told her on the evening of the final, 'I am very proud of you, Alesha. If you win this competition tonight, I will be the happiest nanny in the world.'

The two ladies joined forces in week five of *Strictly*, when Alesha was struggling with the foxtrot. Getting partner Matthew Cutler in a wartime uniform for a tea dance, it was her grandmas who provided the tea and cakes to invoke the perfect forties' tea dance – and told Alesha off for not taking it seriously enough.

Alesha's father Melvin had moved to Thailand by this time and, although she saw little of him in her teen years, Alesha vowed to mend fences with him after her *Strictly* triumph with a four-day visit on her way to promote an album in Japan.

'There is nothing more important to me than my friends and family,' she said.

CHAPTER TWO

Magic and Mis-Teeq

At eighteen, in 1996, Alesha was ready to take on the music world and her confidence was boosted by the Bond Street dancing class where her natural talent was first spotted. 'I started off at the back of the class and by the end I was at the front. I felt I had found something that I really loved,' she told *The Guardian*. 'It unlocked this passion in me that I never knew I had and it just seemed to trigger everything else.'

As Alesha was reaching her early adult years in the quiet suburbs of Welwyn Garden City, the UK garage scene was taking over the clubs of London. The Fridge in Brixton and The Ministry of Sound were adopting this new style of house music and artists such as The Artful Dodger and Shanks and Bigfoot were filling the floors every weekend. The smart music wannabe soon realized she had to broaden her horizons in order to gain the knowledge and influences she needed to make it in this competitive world. Too broke to move out of the family home, Alesha decided that frequent trips to London, either to attend dance classes or to party to the early hours at the many R&B and garage clubs, were absolutely essential.

'I'm from a small town and there's not much opportunity round there and I had to remove myself and travel to people who were into the same things I was into,' she says. 'So to any budding artist I would say, surround yourself with people who've got the same interests as you and have the same music tastes as you, that's very helpful as well.'

As for most musicians, however, success didn't come overnight and Alesha spent four years scraping money together to pay for her club nights and dance lessons. She later admitted to *The Times* that she would dodge fares on trains to get to rehearsals, incurring fines that her mum scrimped to pay. A short spell working at Ladbrokes betting shop helped with the finance for a while, but she spent her days there 'daydreaming about my music career'.

'There were many years I was skint; I had no money in my pocket, just for the love of music,' Alesha told a music website in 2006. 'I could have gone to university but I chose not to because I had faith in what I was doing. And I had part-time jobs just to get money to get on the train literally to get to rehearsals.

'I used to wear the same pair of jeans for months on end and the same pair of trainers for months on end and I used to borrow my friends' clothes. But I didn't care, because I knew that what I was trying to do was bigger than that.'

Once again it was her mum Beverley who stood behind Alesha, backing her decision to drop the university course and keeping her dream alive. 'Just one person having faith in you makes a difference. If you don't have that support system, I don't know how you can do it. I'm sure there are people who have their own reasons for making it, but for me having that one person in my life who supported me one hundred per cent really helped.'

During this lean period, Alesha met a girl who was to change her life forever. Sabrina Washington was born in the same month as Alesha, brought up in a Jamaican family in north west London and shared Alesha's burning ambition to make it as a rap and R&B star.

Unlike Alesha, however, Sabrina had grown up in a musical family, her dad was in a reggae band that played with Buju Banton. At her convent school, Sabrina had set up a rap outfit called 4 By 4 and, despite her mother's wish that she study law, Sabrina was determined that a career as a singer was for her, especially after her group won the Nubian Spotlight Contest at London club The Mean Fiddler.

'It could have all been so different,' recalls Sabrina. 'I wanted to be a barrister as my mum was very keen on education. As it was, I trained as a dental hygienist so I could concentrate on my music. It was 4 By 4 that got me going. Once I won that competition I knew what I wanted.'

Alesha and Sabrina met in 1999 at a Fulham studio called Dance Attic and the bond was instant. 'We were both working on separate projects at the time. But when we met we got along and felt that we could do something together,' Alesha explained. 'I liked her vibe and I think she got a good vibe from me so we hooked up.'

The two girls worked together for over a year before signing up to a production company to help find their sound, and it was during this period that Alesha's husky MC-ing came to the fore. At a show at Earl's Court the production company urged her to include a rap, but the usually ballsy Alesha lost her nerve. 'I really didn't want to do it, because I thought people would laugh at me,' she later revealed to the *I Like Music* website. 'Seriously! I mean at that time I'd not seen female MCs in the UK before, but I did it and the feedback was really good, and from that point

I started developing it and taking it more seriously. Then I'd go to clubs and, when I got the chance, I'd pick up the mike. But the guys didn't want to give me the mike, so I'd just persist and hover around the DJ bit, have a little go and it went on from there.'

Knowing what an impact she could have, Sabrina encouraged Alesha to develop her skills at the mike.

'When she first started she was a bit shy, but I always said that it adds something, an element of difference. It was the first time I'd ever heard a woman MC and I was like, "Alesha, you have to do that," and she was like, "No, Bri, don't make me look stupid."'

The two girls soon began to record a demo album called *Inspiration*, but before they had completed it, the duo became a trio. Su-Elise Nash caught the eye of the two girls when she attended an audition for another girl band at the Dance Attic in 2000. The pretty eighteen-year-old was amazed when Sabrina and Alesha approached her and asked her to join.

'They were rehearsing upstairs, and when they saw me, they asked if I could sing too,' Su-Elise told *The Sun*. 'I said yes and they asked me if I wanted to join them. And that was that.'

Having started a business degree at Middlesex University the bright teenager dropped out to pursue her dream of stardom.

'When me and Sabrina met up it just seemed right to join as a duo,' Alesha explained later. 'Then, when Su-Elise came along it was as if she added the final part.

'We met Su-Elise while Sabrina and me were rehearsing. We told her that we didn't have a deal but asked if she was interested in working with us. We came together in a natural way.'

After months of gruelling rehearsals in the dance studio the trio were signed up by respected dance imprint Inferno and another audition produced a fourth member, Birmingham-born singer Zena McNally. The next few months were spent in the recording studio with various producers, including Norwegian duo Stargate, Ed Case, Rishi Rich and Ceri Evans. Finally, in August 2000, the newly formed quartet launched themselves with the single 'Why?', a moody R&B track co-written and produced by David Brant, which told the story of friends becoming lovers. The track fared poorly until a remix version by Matt 'Jam' Lamont, released in January 2001, speeded up the tempo and gave Alesha her first chance to display the deep, earthy rap style that she had perfected at the mike as a feisty teenager. The remix finally put their names on the map and became a surprise smash in the underground UK garage clubs, prompting the girls to record a second video.

Despite little media support the single reached the ears of Radio One's Dream Team, who championed it as 'bad, bold and sassy', helping it to climb the UK charts where it eventually peaked at number 8. 'When it charted, we were all listening to the Radio One countdown on Sunday at my mum's,' remembers Alesha. 'I started crying, my nan started crying. We were all bawling.'

Surprisingly, just before the band enjoyed their first chart success, Zena bailed and decided to pursue a solo career, signing to Mercury records a year later. Alesha insists the three girls didn't push her out and actually found her sudden departure inconvenient, as the new single showed all four girls on the cover. By the time they achieved a childhood dream, with their first *Top of the Pops* appearance, they were back to being a trio.

'When there were four of us, there was a great buzz and such excitement,' Alesha told *The Guardian* in 2002. 'We all agreed to be positive and go forward together. We didn't kick her out! We had a single out and a video out with four people in them. We looked stupid! But . . . well, there were other issues in her life, and it made us stronger.'

Following Zena's shock exit, Alesha, Sabrina and Su-Elise signed an album deal with the country's biggest independent label, Telstar, who impressed the girls with their commitment to a long-term career. 'Telstar showed faith in us and said they'd make us an album-selling act, not just a one-hit wonder,' says Alesha.

The girls proved the point with their second single, 'All I Want', released in June 2001. Alesha co-wrote the song with David Brant, Maryanne Morgan and Alan M. Glass and it was produced by Ceri Evans aka Sunship. With a faster riff and catchier tune than their debut, 'All I Want' featured an opening rap from Alesha with the lyrics, 'M with the I with the S-T double E Q / All I want is to be with you / Mis-Teeq with the one Sunship, It's time to rock the Party!' The video saw the girls indulge in a childlike fantasy, with Su-Elise disappearing through a full-length mirror, followed by her band mates, to a white and gold stage where the girls strut their stuff with leather-clad dancers.

The single flew into the charts at number 2, prompting, no doubt, more tears of joy in Alesha's family home. Mum Beverley, who had started to collect press cuttings in a scrapbook when her daughter embarked on her career, found herself snipping and gluing with ever-increasing regularity as the media started showing more interest in the three sexy singers.

And they weren't the only ones. As the millennium dawned, another up-and-coming band, the thirty-strong So Solid Crew, were making their mark in the underground clubs and one cocky member of the crew, MC Harvey, was making a beeline for the Mis-Teeq beauty. It wasn't exactly love at first sight.

'We first met in a club in Watford, where both our groups were doing PAs,' Alesha recalled later. 'I didn't really like him. He just seemed a bit too confident. But maybe that was a result of too much alcohol.'

'Harvey was a little bit drunk,' she told *The Observer* magazine. 'We were in the VIP section of this club, and you know what that's like, and I was not the only girl he'd chatted to that night, so I wasn't interested. I'm not stupid. But we kept bumping into each other in different clubs. And then one time he bought me a glass of champagne and we had a dance, and that's when I gave him my number.'

Harvey, real name Mike Harvey, was born and raised in south London and was just slightly younger than Alesha. His family had already had a taste of celebrity when his bodybuilder dad, who shares his name, starred as Bullit in the live arena version of the TV contest *Gladiators*.

As Mis-Teeq's singles began climbing to the top ten, So Solid Crew were hitting the top spot with their August 2001 single, '21 Seconds'. At the same time, the activities of a few of the members of the crew, as well as their controversial lyrics, were causing a storm in the media, who accused them of glamorizing violence. But Alesha kept bumping into Harvey at TV studios and nightclubs and she began to like what she saw. The pair were soon inseparable and Harvey began to encourage Alesha and support her as she further developed her distinctive style and dealt with the rise of the band. Unlike many of the male MCs at the time, Harvey liked Alesha's style. 'I used to go to clubs like Twice As Nice and the guys wouldn't give me the mike. They'd look at me in my sexy dress and think, "What the hell can she do?" With Harvey, it was the opposite. He was proud of me.'

The newly besotted Harvey helped Alesha develop her style and she began to try out her MC lyrics on him. 'When Harvey first heard my MC-ing, being an MC himself, he always said I had potential, but there was a lot of things I could improve on. One day he wrote me a lyric. Sometimes I'd write something and I'd ask him what he thought, and he'd say, "That bit sounds a bit dodgy. Switch up your flow," or whatever.'

Although much of the UK garage scene hailed from the gang-land streets of London, Alesha and her band-mates were keen to show the less controversial side of urban music. 'Don't promote violence but talk about life,' Alesha said in a BBC interview. 'Talk about where you've come from, where you're going and what you've been through, but be careful how you put things across.'

As the buzz surrounding the three beauties increased in volume, one of the UK's top comedians sat up and took notice. Sacha Baron Cohen was busy working on his first feature film, starring his cheeky interviewer Ali G, and was keen to persuade Mis-Teeq to join his 'Staines Massive'.

'We have been approached by Sacha and we're doing a song for the soundtrack,' Sabrina revealed in the *Daily Star* in October 2001. 'We all think that Ali G's wicked and we're all massive fans. When we're less busy, we'll settle down and go into a recording studio and record the song. We'll have to see what we can pull off – but whatever happens, the song's going to be very interesting.' Despite rumours that the song would be penned by Sacha himself, Mis-Teeq went on to record a cover version of the Montel Jordan hit, 'This Is How We Do It' for the release of *Ali G Indahouse* in 2002.

Back in the summer of 2001, with just two top-ten singles under their belts, the trio were voted Artist of the Year at the UK Garage Awards and were thrilled to be nominated for two awards at the 2001 MOBO (Music of Black Origin) Awards. In the Best Newcomer category they found themselves up against So Solid's Oxide & Neutrino, India Arie and DJ Pied Piper & the Masters of Ceremonies and, for Best UK Act, they were battling with the likes of Sade, Damage and the platinum-selling artist Craig David. As Alesha and Harvey had only just started dating, it must have raised a wry smile when they discovered that So Solid Crew were also major contenders for both gongs.

As a nominated act, Mis-Teeq was invited to perform at the ceremony that October, which was an incredible opportunity for such a new band. Just eight months after they signed the album deal, the girls had hit the big time – and they were stunned. 'It does seem a little crazy,' said Alesha. 'Performing at the MOBOs? Weird. But we have worked hard.' Band-mate Sabrina reiterated the point that the girls had been through a gruelling year to claw their way to this prestigious reward. 'We all have long-term boyfriends who have been around since before the band. But it has been hard to see them because of all the work we have had to put in. It is gruelling. But we are determined to make this work.'

At the ceremony, the group lost out to Craig David for Best UK Act and saw Harvey's Crew pick up the Best Newcomer award, along with the Best UK Garage Act. But Mis-Teeq wowed the audience and the press alike with a performance of 'All I Want', dressed in scarlet tracksuits and perched on powerful red motorbikes. Had there been an award for the UK's sexiest girl band, they would have clinched it there and then.

'That's all been fantastic. We're very proud,' said Su-Elise Nash. 'We've watched the MOBOs since it first started and we've always thought we'd love to be there, we'd love to perform there, but to actually be asked to perform and get two nominations, plus four nominations at the UK Garage Awards is just great — it's recognition for what we're doing.'

'It's a really surreal feeling for us,' commented Alesha. 'This time last year we wouldn't have envisaged that we'd be in this position at all. It's a wicked feeling to know that we are representing the UK, we feel we're the first urban/garage girl group and up there representing feels good.'

The triumphant trio followed their chart success with a third single, 'One Night Stand'. As before, the video started with a little acting from the girls, showing them getting ready for a night out and nagging Sabrina to hurry up. Their plush surroundings in an up-market flat and a flash car with the number plate 'Mis-Teeq' seemed to suggest they had left their penniless days behind them and were revelling in their new-found wealth. It even includes a line about trendy tipple Cristal champagne, 'If it ain't Cristal, Mis-Teeq ain't sippin''. But Alesha was never one to forget her roots. While Su-Elise joked, 'I haven't changed, I wore Gucci then, and I wear Gucci now,' Alesha stuck to her high-street clothes and named Karen Millen, Mango and Miss Selfridge as her favourite stores. She would wait for the 'silly money' before splashing out on serious designer gear, she said. In the meantime, all she really wanted to do was treat her mum.

'That's one of the things that is so great about having a bit of money now,' she said in April 2002. 'I'm not on silly money but I have enough to buy her the things that she needs, like a fridge or a rug. It's just nice to be able to give her a bit of cash so she can spend it on herself – she spent so much of her life giving me her money.'

The single reached number 5 in the UK charts and made it into the top forty in Australia, New Zealand, Denmark, Norway and Ireland, signaling that their sound was beginning to register on an international scale.

Two weeks after the release of 'One Night Stand' came the debut album, provocatively titled *Lickin' On Both Sides*. It featured the three hits as well as 'They'll Never know', a collaboration with their new best friends, So Solid Crew, and the first track to feature rap verses with a sung chorus. The Crew's Asher D and Harvey interlaced their own lyrics with Alesha's throaty MC-ing and the song looks back to the humble beginnings of both bands, with Alesha's section referring to the days when she couldn't pay the rent.

'The track is about the struggles we went through to get where we are,' explained Sabrina at the time. 'A lot of people think that Mis-Teeq happened overnight, but it didn't. There were times when I didn't have a pound in my pocket and Alesha found it hard coming up from Welwyn to get into London and she didn't have no money. We were very determined, and we knew what we wanted, but sometimes it was really, really hard. Especially when you didn't have any money and you had to decide between going to your part-time job to earn money, or going to an audition or a showcase for a record company that you really needed to be at.'

'People say we have suddenly broken through, but that isn't the case,' said Alesha. 'We've been around for three years now. We've worked hard recording and we only made the deal when we felt we were ready. We signed in December after we recorded "Why?". We felt the time was right.'

Talking about the album, Alesha hinted that the diversity of their influences and the refusal to be pigeon-holed was behind the band's enigmatic name. 'There's lots of R&B, lots of sophisticated garage, hip hop influences, reggae and calypso influences in the album,' said Alesha. 'A mix of everything really. That's what we set out to do, hence our name Mis-Teeq.'

The album was released on 29 October 2001 to rave reviews from the press. The *Sunday Mirror* gave it nine out of ten and *The Guardian* gushed, 'The music slides down as fizzily as their favourite tipple. That, of course, is Cristal champagne!' The reviewer singled out Alesha, saying she, 'shines brightest of the three, with her ability to slip from silky singing to ragga-girl rapping. A cavalcade of trendy producers, including their So Solid mates, was involved, but the sound is as distinctive as anything you'll find in R&B.'

Lisa Verrico, in *The Times*, dubbed them, 'The Spice Girls of garage,' and declared, 'The first song and current single "One Night Stand", their breakthrough hit "Why?" and Sunship's edit of "All I Want" are dance floor fillers that should stand the test of time. But for this week at least, the Brit girls are on top of America's R&B babes.'

The comparison to the American bands was a pertinent one for the trio, who were constantly being compared to Beyoncé's group Destiny's Child. Every other newspaper article dubbed them 'Britain's answer to Destiny's Child', to the irritation of the girls.

'We're Mis-Teeq!' Su-Elise told one journalist who mentioned the rival divas. 'We're versatile; a mixture; a crossover – R&B into garage.'

Sabrina was equally firm when asked about their American counterparts, 'We're not Destiny's Child. They're Texan church girls and we're British club kids from the garage underground. It's two different worlds,' she said. 'We're British and proud of it. Our music has a distinctive, British feel and we like to think we have a distinctive, British look.'

'We don't want to sound American,' insisted Alesha. 'We're part of a generation that doesn't have to look to the US for inspiration.'

'Look, people like to compare you,' she told the *Sunday Express*. 'If we were three white girls, they'd probably say we're like Atomic Kitten. People are bound to think, "Three black girls, they're just like Destiny's Child," but they come from Texas, from a gospel church background, while we're from the UK, from a garage underground scene.'

In fact the girls' sound was very different from the smooth R&B vocals of Destiny's Child, using a mixture of R&B, garage, ragga and hip-hop. 'When you go out to a rave, you have a garage room and an R&B room,' explained Su-Elise to the uninitiated. 'They go hand-in-hand on the London club scene, which is where we're coming from. We just make music, there don't have to be rules.'

Lickin' On Both Sides went double platinum, selling over 600,000 copies and, in the UK at least, by the end of 2001, Mis-Teeq had made the big time. They performed at the club haven of Ayia Napa, appeared on numerous TV shows and rounded off the year with their first live London gig, on 14 December, at

La Scala in King's Cross. With only one album to their name they still managed to belt out forty minutes of their album tracks, to high praise from the music critics.

'The high tempos and ragga-style syncopations that make UK garage the most exciting music in Britain today can really bring a crowd to life,' said *The Daily Telegraph*. 'And in twenty-two-year-old Alesha Dixon the group have an MC and rapper instinctively in tune with its stop-start dynamics. Elegant and willowy, but seemingly in perpetual motion, Dixon was a blur of red tassels and high-speed patois, linking the trio effortlessly with the backing band and DJ, over whose soundtrack they layered their soaring voices. MC-ing tends to be a man's world, but Dixon balanced gruffness and feminine allure with aplomb.'

Alesha had arrived.

CHAPTER THREE

Solid Stardom

Mis-Teeq were not only gaining a reputation as the hottest girl band in the business, but also the nicest. The press raved about their sunny natures, their fans adored them and they were making friends among their contemporaries on the music scene.

'We're particularly friendly to everyone because we care and we're not too big for our boots,' Alesha explained. It made good business sense too and the girls were all too aware that, in the music world, what goes up may well come down.

'The people you mistreat on the way up could be the ones to help you on the way down,' said Sabrina. 'So it's nice to be level-headed.'

As the UK garage scene continued to dominate the clubs and airwaves of the country, Mis-Teeq and So Solid Crew stood out as the most mainstream acts, with their urban anthems enjoying the chart success few underground acts had achieved in the past. The thirty-strong collective whose original line-up included rappers MC Romeo, Asher D and garage diva Lisa Maffia followed their number one hit, '21 Seconds', with 'They Don't Know'.

The song, which became a precursor to Mis-Teeq's collaboration with the group on 'They'll Never Know', again harks back to the days the members had nothing, with Asher D rapping, 'Back in the day, I had no luxury'. The track reached number 3 in the charts and their debut album, with the same name, flew in at number 6. But the group's rise to fame was steeped in controversy, and Mis-Teeq's association with So Solid Crew, strengthened by Alesha's blossoming romance with Harvey, threw a shadow over Mis-Teeq's spotless reputation.

Asher D, real name Ashley Walters, was arrested in July 2001 after an argument with a traffic warden and was found to be carrying a loaded air pistol. He was later sentenced to eighteen months. MC Neutrino, aka Mark Oseitutu, was arrested and released without charge after being shot in the leg outside a London club in May and Skat D, real name Darren Weir, admitted breaking the jaw of a fifteen-year-old girl who spurned his advances.

To make matters worse, two people were shot and injured during the group's gig at the Astoria in London, in November 2001, forcing police and promoters to cancel the entire UK tour.

'I think the whole thing has been blown out of proportion,' Alesha told *The Sun*. 'They're not the painted picture the media likes to create. Trouble happens everywhere in the country in all types of music.

'We've not had any trouble ourselves, but we're not stupid girls. We know that where there's love there's hate, and where there's praise there's people dissing you. People are entitled to their opinion. It takes two to make a fight, doesn't it?'

Even so, she knew the stories reflected badly on her boyfriend and was quick to point out that he was not a gun-toting gangsta. 'So Solid were being vilified at the time, but Harvey's not a violent man. He didn't want to be tarred with that brush. That's why he left before they made their second album.'

However, Harvey did return to perform with them, and even Alesha admitted to *The Daily Telegraph*, in February 2002, that she found So Solid crowds intimidating and was staying away from Harvey's gigs. 'Harvey was very upset that the tour was stopped, especially for people who had already bought tickets. But I think they'll come back and do a bigger tour than the one that got cancelled.

'You do get troublemakers. I think maybe these people have come from a similar environment to So Solid and they don't like seeing them up there, doing well.

And it's not only about So Solid gigs. We just don't go out to certain places. Raving in general has got dangerous, and now I'll really only go and see Harvey at university dates. Go to one of those and the crowd is lovely. I don't bother with places where people are trying to make you feel intimidated and uncomfortable.'

She even confessed that she would think twice before letting a child of hers go to a So Solid date. 'I think it's up to the individual parent, though to be honest I have my doubts. But you know, So Solid are just putting on a stage performance – they are just an act.'

While band members Su-Elise and Sabrina were happy with their long-term boyfriends from outside the industry, Alesha and Harvey became the king and queen of the scene. One newspaper called them the 'Posh and Becks of UK garage' and they were every bit as loved up.

'I wouldn't say that our relationship has helped [our careers],' Harvey told *The Observer*. 'We're looked at as an urban couple, in the limelight, but the relationship has not helped our profile. Our profile might have made our relationship a lot stronger, a lot quicker, but that is it.'

And while the street-smart So Solid Crew were being pilloried in the press for promoting violence, Alesha was making busy ruining Harvey's reputation as a south London hard man with such statements as, 'We'd rather sit at home and have a cup of tea than go to a rave.'

Also, while they loved to practise quick-fire rapping over the sounds of MTV, Alesha and Harvey avoided being seen out too often at showbiz parties. Their relationship, they insisted, was not about being seen but about genuine passions. 'Unconditional love,' gushed Alesha. 'That's what we're trying to create here.'

'I love him,' she confessed to *The Observer* in June 2002. 'Last night I was on the computer for about two hours and he was upstairs cleaning my room. When I came out of the living room there was a sign in the doorway that said, "Follow Love" and as I got to the top of the stairs, it said, "Getting close". When I went into my room, there was a sign in front of my bed that said, "Harvey loves Alesha", with a picture of me and I just started cracking up.'

She also revealed she was still in the phase of dating where she liked to look her best for her boyfriend, and told an endearing tale of a recent meeting. 'After we came back from our last promo trip I was desperate to see him and I couldn't get hold of him. I was having dinner with the girls. I was so depressed I hadn't even brushed my hair, and who walks in the door? Harvey! I couldn't believe it. I put my head in my dinner.'

After nearly a year of dating, Alesha revealed that the couple had plans to move in together but were both worried about leaving their mums! 'MC lives with his mum and I live with my mum. We are looking for somewhere of our own, but Harvey loves staying at my mum's house because after growing up in London, Hertfordshire seems very peaceful.'

For an artist so much in demand, success often comes at a price. Increased popularity inevitably leads to a fuller diary and precious time with Harvey had to be snatched between gigs, public appearances and recordings. Harvey helped Alesha cope with her burgeoning fame and even toured with her as she struggled to deal with her new status as pop queen. 'For six months, I lived in her world,' he said.

In February 2001, Mis-Teeq announced that they would tour with reggae artist Shaggy, of 'Boombastic' and 'It Wasn't Me' fame, and released a statement expressing their delight at this opportunity. 'To be supporting an artist like Shaggy, who reaches young, old, whites and blacks, is something special,' it read.

'We met Shaggy briefly at the Smash Hits Awards and, after he saw us perform live there, he asked if we would be his support for the tour, which was incredible,' Su-Elise revealed. 'I mean, we are playing huge arenas, the sort of venue I used to go to see all my idols but which I never thought I'd be performing in myself.'

At the same time they were basking in the glow of a BRIT Awards nomination as Best Newcomer, working on the track for Sacha Baron Cohen's *Ali G Indahouse* movie and promoting their fourth single, 'B With Me'. The fast-tempo dance track about forbidden love and office romance featured a Kalashnikov speed rap from Alesha and a video that upped the sizzle factor a few notches. After making it into the top ten of the Sexiest Stars in Pop in a *Smash Hits* poll of 900,000 readers, behind Rachel

Stevens, Kylie Minogue and Jennifer Lopez, Alesha raised the temperature by bumping and grinding in tiny denim shorts, a bikini-style top and killer heels, displaying a toned midriff that was the envy of the majority of British women. With straightened and lightened hair completing the new look, Alesha took centre stage in the video as she cavorted with several dancers against a stunning tropical backdrop.

'I've always been a firm believer you can be sexy, but covered,' she said in behind-the-scenes footage of the event. 'So when I saw the clothes for this I was shocked. The director wanted us to wear knickers but we extended it to shorts because it's supposed to be summer, we're walking along the beach and when we get into the shack, and it's night-time, we're wearing denim catsuits, something with a bit more fizz.'

The single matched the success of 'One Night Stand', with a number 5 position in the UK charts, but failed to make any impact internationally. The band were still to crack the toughest nut of all, recognition across the water in the United States, where Destiny's Child, the Texan trio they were so often compared with, dominated the R&B charts.

'America, obviously, is the ultimate dream,' Sabrina told the *Daily Mirror*. 'But we are working so hard here, we want to build on what we have done. We have also been all over Europe and have just got back from Australia. We are going to tour at the end of the year. But next year? Who knows.'

Growing up in a household where money was incredibly tight, Alesha could never afford the slavish following of fashion in which wealthier peers indulged. Instead, she developed her own distinctive look, using whatever she could beg, borrow or afford to buy and, with a body that looks good in anything and an innate sense of style, she became more trendsetter than fashion victim. Success and money meant she could afford to splash out a little more, even if she still stuck to the cheaper end of the market. And the ever-elegant ladies of Mis-Teeq avoided the obvious gangsta girl look. Not for them the ghetto glitter of huge gold earrings and dripping chains favoured by other urban groups eager to show off their newfound wealth.

'We're not bling-bling,' Alesha told *The Observer*. 'That's just a stigma created by the media.' But while she still shunned the high-end designers, she had discovered a new passion for shopping. 'Give us twenty minutes and we'll go shopping,' she said. 'The best one was when we were in Paris at a record-company thing and we literally had half an hour. All of us just ran to the shops and were dashing around Morgan. We had been craving shopping and we were late for the dinner.'

Where pop babes go, the females of the nation will follow, and the band's eye-popping combination of midriff tops, minis and knee-high boots was soon being worn by half the teenage population. High Street stores tapped into the look and everywhere they went kids were emulating their style.

'It's such an amazing thing,' said Sabrina in *The Observer*. 'You would never have thought a year ago that people would want to look like Mis-Teeq, or wear boots because they like Mis-Teeq.'

It soon became clear that the majority of the Mis-Teeq fans were under the age of twenty and that they had spotted something genuine and aspirational in the three women who had pulled themselves up by their high-heeled bootstraps and hip-thrusted their way to a better lifestyle. Alesha turned the youngsters' adoration to her advantage, declaring in one interview, 'Children these days aren't stupid. They like the real-ness of music and can tell when something's manufactured. Whatever we do, people can tell that we enjoy the music we make, that we're in the studio writing our material. That shines through, the same with So Solid, I guess. It comes from us rather than what other people are formulating. Kids know better. They can spot a fake.'

February brought the BRIT Awards, where they would battle for Best Newcomer with the likes of Atomic Kitten, Blue, Damon Albarn's Gorillaz, Starsailor and, of course, So Solid Crew, as well as performing 'One Night Stand' live at the Earl's Court ceremony.

'I don't think we're going to win,' Su-Elise told *The Daily Telegraph* before the ceremony. 'So Solid are also nominated and they won three MOBO awards. Then there's Gorillaz. But I can't wait to do our song. I can't believe we're on the same bill as Sting and Elton John.'

However their performance of 'One Night Stand' that night came with a twist. To please both their mainstream fans and garage club-goers they fused both versions of the song and caused a sensation.

'We didn't set out to steal the show,' said Sabrina. 'We just wanted to do something that people would remember.'

Sadly, Su-Elise's prediction was right on the button and the group went home empty-handed as Blue picked up the gong. So Solid Crew, who performed a blazing set of the two songs culminating in a firework display, landed the Best Video for '21 Seconds'.

The triumphant tour with reggae idol Shaggy, which was extended from six dates to nine, was followed by a scattering of barn-storming Easter gigs, beginning at the Shepherd's Bush Empire, which had *The Independent*'s Simon Price declare, 'This is the sound of High Street Britain 2002.'

Maddy Costa, writing in *The Guardian*, was fascinated by the group's enraptured young audience and the fact that, despite the bumping beats and the rapid-fire MC-ing, very few were dancing. 'Even when the muscular backing musicians rattle out the jittery rhythms of their Ayia Napa hit "All I Want", the audience is rigid, riveted by the trio on stage. You feel the predominantly teenage crowd, who could have walked from the fashion pages of *Mizz* magazine, clocking every move, making mental notes so that they can recreate the show later in their bedrooms. Mis-Teeq are becoming pop idols – and they couldn't appear more delighted with the way their career is progressing.'

Indeed the girls were flying high and loving every minute. The underground scene was firmly behind them and their unique sound was becoming familiar to people of all ages and all walks of life.

'We love to take our music to the widest possible audience,' explained Su-Elise. '*Lickin' on Both Sides*, our album, went platinum last year. We did Radio One roadshows, Party in the Park and appeared on *Top of the Pops* five times.

'We got three MOBO nominations and won Best Act at the UK Garage Awards. And we're learning all the time.'

But the planting of their pedicured feet firmly in the mainstream inevitably brought criticism from the hardline underground artists. The release of the fifth single, the Ali G soundtrack leader 'This Is How We Do It', saw some purists accusing Mis-Teeq of selling out.

'People can say what they like,' said a defensive Su-Elise. 'They might think that crossing over means selling out, but it's more about broadening your audience.'

'There shouldn't be any rules,' added Alesha. 'We're accessible both to clubbers and three-year-olds dancing around their bedrooms.'

Away from the whirlwind of press interviews and live performances, Alesha's romance with Harvey was proving So Solid. Garage's golden couple moved into a flat in Clapham and, after a well-earned break in Fuertaventura in early April 2002, Harvey popped the question. The delighted singer set about arranging an engagement party in Hertfordshire for close friends and family, and Harvey splashed out on an extremely expensive ring.

'I was broke for two months afterwards but it was well worth it,' he said some time later. 'It's the sparkliest thing I've ever bought – all diamonds.'

CHAPTER FOUR

Eye Candy

In terms of social standing, it's a long way from a council house in Welwyn Garden City to the gardens of Buckingham Palace. But on 3 June 2002, the twenty-three-year-old Alesha Dixon found herself on the bill of the Queen's Golden Jubilee concert. As well as the chance to meet members of the Royal Family, she would be performing alongside rock royalty, including Paul McCartney, Brian May, Elton John and Tom Jones. Dame Shirley Bassey was there and Dame Edna Everage provided some comedic entertainment.

Mis-Teeq were set to perform a duet with Ricky Martin, and Alesha was overwhelmed by the scale of the event. 'There was a moment when we'd just finished our sound check and I sat out in the seats where the audience would be; the audience wasn't in yet,' she later recalled on the *I Like Music* website. 'And it was a beautiful summer's day, and on the big screens at the side of the stage, we could see outside the palace where all the crowds were gathering and Paul McCartney was doing a sound check, and me and my TV plugger Laura, we started crying!

'It was one of those surreal moments; Paul McCartney was doing a sound check, we were in the palace getting ready to perform, and we knew how many people around the world were going to be watching and saw the crowds. It was one of those moments, it was really powerful. I'll never forget that.'

Party at the Palace was certainly the biggest audience the band would ever play to, with 12,000 ticket-holders, chosen by lottery, crowding the grounds, an estimated one million watching from the Mall or at the Queen Victoria Memorial, and around 200 million viewers on television. The culmination of a long weekend of Jubilee celebrations, it followed an earlier Music Live push when 200 bands around the country had played 'All You Need Is Love' simultaneously.

Despite her awe at the occasion, the sassy singer couldn't resist a cheeky comment to the Duke of Edinburgh, when he picked her out of an artists' line-up. Wearing very little, as the evening chill began to intrude on a hot summer's day, the Duke approached her and asked, 'Aren't you cold, dear?' Her irreverent riposte was typical of Alesha's no-boundaries attitude. 'What are you going to do? Lend me your jacket, then?' she asked him. 'That's one of my fondest memories,' she later told *The Daily Telegraph*.

'Growing up in Hertfordshire, the pop world could have been Mars. It looked untouchable, another dimension. But standing on stage, waiting to shake hands with the Royal Family, it suddenly hit me, the size of the show and the calibre of artists and, "Oh my God, we're here! We're a part of this!" It was a beautiful moment. Just to get my nan in Buckingham Palace doors was great. She's such a royalist. Me and the girls were more excited about meeting Harry and William.'

The girls continued to ride the wave through a summer of festivals, picking up numerous awards along the way. They were named Best Band at the Maxim Woman of the Year Awards, the Best Dance Act at the Capital FM London Awards and garnered nominations for Best Garage Act and UK Act of the Year at the

2002 MOBOs. At the end of June they switched leather boots for wellies and played a 100,000-strong crowd at Glastonbury, and followed that with sets at the Creamfields Festival in Cheshire and Party in the Park in London's Hyde Park.

'Everything is so full on at the moment,' gasped Alesha. 'We can't believe what's happened. This time last year we were doing small shows and no one had any idea who we were – and now we are playing Glastonbury. It's so amazing.'

Even more amazing for the wide-eyed twenty-three-year-old was being asked to present the MOBO Awards in October with her idol, L L Cool J. Craig David, the Sugababes, Ms Dynamite and Dave Stewart were set to perform on the night and the ceremony promised to be the most glittering in the history of the MOBOs. 'I'm excited and nervous,' Alesha told *The Sun* in the run-up to the evening. 'It's one of the biggest events in the British music calendar, so it is an honour to be asked to present it. It will be nerve-racking to stand up in front of everybody in the industry but I'm doing it for the viewers at home watching and the people who buy our records. I'm doing it for the real fans who have supported and encouraged us as artists.

'I am really excited about meeting LL Cool J because I've been a big fan of his for such a long time. I was listening to his records when I was fifteen, and his new single 'Luv You Better' is one of my favourite tunes at the moment. I have got so much respect for him – so many of his tunes have inspired our group.'

MC Harvey would join her on stage to present one of the awards and the night was to be the jewel in the crown of the King and Queen of UK garage. Alesha had four killer outfits lined up for the evening and the icing on the cake came when

Mis-Teeq scooped the award for the Best Garage Act, and touchingly dedicated it to So Solid Crew.

The sweet gesture would certainly have been a message from Alesha to Harvey, who had been very much on her mind at that time. Absence makes the heart grow fonder, as the old cliché goes, and while Harvey had been at home working on material for his solo album, the trio had been in the States for a month working on their second album, as well as attempting to promote themselves overseas. At the end of their stint abroad, Alesha was missing her man so much she flew straight to Mexico where he was enjoying a holiday with some pals.

'If I hadn't gone I'd have gone mad because I hadn't seen him for three weeks,' she said. 'We stayed in a really nice hotel. We didn't really go out clubbing, we just turned off the mobile phones and chilled.'

With the engagement ring sparkling on Alesha's finger, the couple were constantly being asked when the big day would be. Their reticence even had some asking if everything was still cool between them and whether they would get married at all. But with a punishing schedule, working on the album during the day and often performing at night, it was merely a case of trying to find the time.

'Everything is fantastic with me and Harvey, we can't wait to get married,' the singer told *The Sun*. 'The only factor is our schedules. As soon as we find some time to get married we will. I don't think it will be this year though.'

The dawning of the twenty-first century brought about a new era in celebrity. With the advent of reality shows like *Big Brother*, being famous had become an end in itself, and the hottest spots were full of so-called celebs getting drunk, flashing their underwear and falling out of cabs, in the desperate hope of a paparazzi shot ending up in the tabloids. For three young girls who suddenly had cash to flash, the opportunity to party every night could have been tempting, but Mis-Teeq were rarely seen in a club and, apart from awards ceremonies and personal appearances, they were more likely to be found curled up on the sofa at home. Despite their professed love of Cristal champagne, the showbiz party circuit was not for them.

'A lot of people think that being in the music industry is just about getting dressed up,' said Sabrina, who was engaged to childhood sweetheart Ian Mitchell. 'And a lot of people think that we're quite boring because we don't do the usual showbiz things. They've got to realize that we didn't grow up with that. We grew up away from it and it's an industry we wanted to get into despite all it entailed, but our focus has always been our music.

'Our music came out before anyone had actually seen us, so that's always going to be the main focus for us.'

At the time, Alesha would rather spend her evenings chilling with Harvey than running around West End clubs, and she admitted the work that she loved could be pretty exhausting. 'If you have a hard day at work the first thing you want to do is go home and relax. This is our profession and sometimes people don't understand how many hours you have to put in. We can do a twenty-hour day and that's unheard of in any other profession . . . most people do 9 to 5 with a lunch break. People don't understand that the thing you look forward to most is going home, because you don't see your home.'

At the end of 2002, Mis-Teeq were still riding high, with big plans for their second album, *Eye Candy*. Their month in the

States working with writers and producers was designed to make the album more US friendly, with an eye to climbing up the *Billboard* charts and following Craig David into the mainstream music scene there.

'We've come back from America with three really great songs so it was definitely worth the trip,' said Alesha. 'We had meetings with people in New York and they are definitely feeling our sound over there. There's been some good feedback. Our style will always be the foundation of what we love – R&B, hip-hop, ragga, garage-based music.

'People are still going to hear the Mis-Teeq sound but it's going to be more mature and better because we've grown up. We've really taken the writing by the reins this time and we are feeling more confident and free. The nicest thing is Sabrina, Su and me are just having a good time together.'

Harvey, however, was not finding life without his 'Crew' as easy as he supposed. Having attempted to distance himself from the violent image of the group, he signed a solo deal and released his first single, 'Get Up And Move', which featured the repeated lyric 'Thou shalt not kill' while focusing on life in 'the ghetto'. The single, released in September 2002, reached number 24 in the charts and, in January 2003, his record company, Go! Beat, pulled the plug on his solo album and dropped him from their books.

Although he returned to perform with So Solid Crew, and signed up to join them at the Brits in February, the unexpected blow made him rethink and reevaluate his future.

Another shadow over Mis-Teeq's runaway success came at Christmas 2002, with the death of their tour manager. As Alesha and Harvey celebrated with a round of family get-togethers,

John McMahon, who also looked after Girls Aloud, Craig David and Ms Dynamite, was killed after his people carrier careered off the road in Staffordshire. 'We are deeply shocked,' said Sabrina in a statement. 'John was a lovely man who will be sorely missed by us and everyone he worked with. Our thoughts are with John's family.'

As work on the new album drew to a close, Mis-Teeq and So Solid both lost out at the BRITs when south London star Ms Dynamite walked away with the Best Urban Act award. But, after a gap of nearly nine months since their last single, the girls' next move was about to prove a humdinger.

The release of 'Scandalous' in March showed a more sophisticated sound and a definite shift towards the R&B end of the scale, away from the hard garage sound of their first album. Alesha's solo sections were softened, with a sing-song style somewhere between full vocals and rap, and the track opened with an acknowledgement of their mainstream, catchy appeal and a message to rival bands. 'You know you wanna sing with us. That's why you know you should be scared of us.'

The Daily Mirror called the single, 'the best thing to hit the airwaves in ages' and Coca-Cola used it as the backing for their latest ad, with the girls starring as themselves alongside Busted and Kym Marsh.

As the release hit the shops, Alesha got her first big TV break as a presenter, with an opportunity to front the Saturday morning show *SM:TV Live* with Tess Daly and Brian Dowling.

'Scandalous' matched their biggest hit to date, climbing to number 2 in the charts and only being kept off the top spot by the Comic Relief single, 'Spirit In The Sky', performed by Gareth Gates and the Kumars. Internationally, it became their biggest hit, entering the top twenty in Australia, New Zealand and all over Europe and even cracking the precious Billboard Charts in the States, albeit at number 35. The following year it was to give the girls an even higher profile over the water when the track was chosen for the soundtrack of Halle Berry's blockbuster *Batman* spin-off, *Catwoman*.

The garage goddesses were surprised and delighted by the reaction to the track. 'That one will be a tough act to follow,' said Su-Elise. 'We loved it ourselves, but didn't expect it to go quite so crazy as it did. We are doing some work in the studio at the moment, and we are concentrating on laying down some new tracks to be used as singles.'

The single was followed shortly afterwards by the release of the long-awaited second album, *Eye Candy*, on 31 March. After seven months of hard slog recording the album, Mis-Teeq were justifiably proud of what they had produced. With production by Stargate, who had featured heavily on *Lickin' On Both Sides,* as well as Salaam Remi, Grammy Award-winning American singer Joe, and sought-after US record producer Jermaine Dupri.

The long wait from third single to second album may have been unusual for a band so hungry for hits, but Alesha said that after their initial success they had really wanted to sit back and smell the roses. 'After we released "Why?" there was a buzz around us which just intensified through the singles and it was hard to have time to think,' she told the *Daily Record* in Scotland. 'We released the last single in June or July last year and then wanted to step back and prepare for phase two. 2001 to 2002 was such a great time. So much happened and we wanted time to look back and say: "Wow". Too many artists just keep on going and then years later can't remember all these amazing things, people and places they met as it's all a blur.'

She also revealed that the record company had wanted Mis-Teeq to bring the new album out before Christmas, but they had stood their ground because they wanted it to be the best possible follow-up to *Lickin' On Both Sides.* 'We asked for a couple more months to write the best we could – to get the music right and exactly what we wanted. No artist can afford to take the risk and we want to be different – and the only way to do that is to develop your sound, not just churn stuff out.

'We want to release three albums and carry on, not implode and split up before the third one is released, like so many British female groups.'

Many of the reviewers agreed that the extra time had paid off.

'The garage girl group have hooked up with a string of top producers to make this 15-track CD, which is set to be a huge hit,' said *The Sun*, praising the album's 'stacks of catchy tunes'.

'Mis-Teeq place a sassy, distinctly British slant on the female harmonies of American girl groups such as Destiny's Child,' said the *Daily Mail*, giving it five stars. The girls, said the review, 'combine dance rhythms and pop with such effortless vim and vigour that they could soon supplant Atomic Kitten and the Sugababes as our leading girl group. Current single "Scandalous" sets the tone with its staccato beats, police sirens and vibrant vocals while "Can't Get It Back" is also impressively indignant. But Mis-Teeq are also happy to try a little tenderness – "Beginning To Feel Like Love" is a superbly sung ballad.'

However, as with 'Scandalous', the softer vocals on all the tracks, with the exception of heavy dance anthem 'Nitro', had deliberately distanced the sound from the underground urban scene, toned down Alesha's earthy MC-ing and moved the band more into the mainstream. Not everybody approved.

'Despite giving a thank-you sent out to "the Gucci massive" in the album credits, the follow-up to *Lickin' On Both Sides* is a grab-bag of high-street bling lite: exactly the sort of teeny pop that you would expect from a trio of girls who dot the "i" in their name with a little heart,' said *The Times'* review. 'While they may have scooped the award for Best Garage Act at last year's MOBOs, Mis-Teeq steer clear of Ms Dynamite's urban proselytizing: tracks such as "Dance Your Cares Away" and "Best Friends" bottle pop fizz with a generous twist of saccharine sentiment, leaving only "Nitro" to flirt with hardcore beats and ragga.' The reviewer did, however, concede that the singles, 'Scandalous' and the forthcoming 'Can't Get It Back' 'both aim high and hit the mark'.

Nonetheless, the girls were confident they could achieve more with their second album and set about selling themselves. 'We're looking forward to more success this year,' said Sabrina. 'And I hope we can live up to people's expectations.'

The shift towards purer R&B meant the Destiny's Child comparisons kept on coming, much to Sabrina's disgust. 'We are not Destiny's Child,' she said. 'If anything I would rather be compared with Christina Aguilera. I think she is great. I'm really looking forward to seeing her play live. She puts on a great show and she can really blow!'

In a bid to conquer the overseas markets, Mis-Teeq signed on to the books of PR giants Freud Communications and spent months in a frenzy of CD signings, record-store appearances and live performances. Aware that their attempts to crack the

US market might be seen as selling out their UK fanbase, Alesha was quick to explain and was brutally honest about their motives. 'When we do go to America, people will just have to accept that we're going,' she told *The Daily Telegraph*. 'As much as the general public think you're rich, let's be straight: you can't get rich in England.

'If I could become a millionaire just by selling records at home, that's what I'd do – I could stay with my family and just go on holiday to America once in a while. But we're going to be here for quite a bit longer yet.'

And despite their use of US producers on the album, the band were keen to big up the home-grown talent. 'It's a great time for British music in general,' said Sabrina. 'It's getting very much tighter, production-wise. In the US, they've always been on point with vocals, on point with production, but now we've got a lot of fantastic producers coming out of the UK, people elsewhere are starting to take notice of the fact that the British can do it, too.'

Unfortunately, despite the endorsement from catwoman herself, Mis-Teeq's single and album failed to make any real impact in the States. In the UK, however, *Eye Candy* reached number 6 in the charts but didn't quite live up to the sales of *Lickin' On Both Sides*, going single platinum rather than double.

In the whirlwind of publicity, the girls were suffering from lack of sleep and had precious little time off. With all three now sporting engagement rings, they were struggling to find time with their respective fiancés and getting fed up with speculation about their forthcoming nuptials. Stories that they were plan-ning a triple wedding kept cropping up and they even stopped going out in public together with their partners.

'We have been away touring so much that we haven't had any time to spend with our partners,' said Sabrina in the *Daily Star*. 'Now we've got to find more time to spend with them and we're hoping it's going to be quality time! All we do when we're not working is sleep. We just need to recover from our hectic schedules.'

And Alesha revealed that her elusive wedding date was still buried under a pile of work commitments. 'We haven't had a chance to set a date yet,' she said. 'I want to be able to say: "Yeah, we're going to get married next month, or even in six months." But the next thing you know we're being told you've got to work on this and that, fly to LA or you're going on a tour. Me and Harvey are cool and can't wait to be married. But sometimes I really do wonder if it's ever going to happen. We just never seem to have any time.'

The last thing she wanted was to rush her big day, or go for a quickie ceremony abroad. 'I'd have to have my friends and family there. I'm not yet rich enough to fly them all to Las Vegas.'

CHAPTER FIVE

Hip Hop Style

Looking back on the band's next single, Alesha may well allow herself a bitter smile. 'Can't Get It Back', released in July 2003, is a defiant message to a cheating husband. A verse that sets the scene with the words 'We got engaged to be married the very next May,' is followed by a chorus that declares, 'Now the ring that you gave me/ You can't get it back.' Once again, Alesha delivers her own inimitable rhyme about a cheating husband which, just three years later, would prove horribly portentous.

Whether or not the three happily engaged ladies intended the song as a warning to their husbands-to-be, in retrospect it certainly looks like a premonition of Alesha's troubles. The video was even closer to the future truth, although it was Sabrina who plays the divorcee, tearing a picture of herself and her former spouse in half before appearing in a divorce court in front if a doddery old judge.

The band went for comedy value in the promo, having the well-ordered court descend into chaos as the gorgeous girls, dressed in skintight clothes, accuse the defendant of cheating. Bras land on the shocked judge's head and even a court orderly appears to mock the size of the accused's manhood. In cutaway shots, we see the cheating hubby being caught out and then the three vengeful vixens tying him up in his undies leaving him to be found in an office building by a lusty cleaner in rollers.

As the courtroom is adjourned the judge rises to reveal he is wearing union jack boxer shorts behind the desk.

The light, bubbly single, with a catchy chorus, failed to reach the heights of its predecessor only getting to number 8. Ironically, the number one for most of the month was 'Crazy In Love', Beyoncé's first single without Destiny's Child, on which she collaborated with future husband Jay Z.

In the autumn of 2003, the band embarked on their first full UK tour, warming up with a one-off gig at La Scala in King's Cross, where they had played their first live concert. There, Alesha revealed her rock and roll secret — that the most 'scandalous' things the girls had done was switch their mobile phones off! 'When our manager or the record company are hounding us, we get together and decide to turn our phones off — all at the same time,' she confessed to the *Daily Mirror*. 'It doesn't half wind them up.'

The tour bus hit the road in early September with nineteen dates from Plymouth to Glasgow, and including stopovers in York, Birmingham, Manchester and many more venues around the country. After three years of slogging in studios, the fired-up trio were looking forward to bringing the show to their many fans. And they whet their appetite by promising a gig to remember.

'We can't wait,' Su-Elise told the *Liverpool Echo*. 'It's a chance for us to really show what we can do, to prove ourselves in the live arena. Doing the TV spots and the personal appearances is great in its own way, but it can be very limiting. You are restricted to doing a certain routine in a certain way, whereas live, we are getting the chance to mix it up a bit, to try out some ideas, work creatively with a band as well, which is great for us.'

'Fans can expect a high-energy performance from us,' added Sabrina. 'It won't just be about pyrotechnics – it will be about us and our live show. We have two costume changes and we will be looking quite glitzy.'

The live show, which kicked off in Liverpool, began with luminescent strobes lighting up the excited audience as a voice announced 'You are now entering the Mis-Teeq zone,' prompting screams from the largely teen crowd. The girls ripped through the hits, including 'All I Want', 'B With Me' and, of course, 'Scandalous' as well as a medley of urban covers, including Salt'N'Peppa's 'Push It' which, incidentally, was the first single both Alesha and Sabrina bought. Their sizeable band included a DJ, two guitarists, a drummer, keyboard players and two backing singers, and the group exuded the sort of energy most acts can only dream about mustering.

Beginning the set in sparkly, fringed bras and white combats, they announced the R&B ballad segment with a quick change into red tops and long, semi-transparent skirts before bringing the show to a glamorous close in tiny, diamanté-studded mini-skirts and the inevitable knee-length boots.

As they belted out divorce anthem 'Can't Get It Back', they dragged an unsuspecting male out of the audience to recreate the kidnap scene in the video, tied him to a chair and gave him a sexy lap dance. Strangely enough, there were no complaints from any of the 'victims' involved. At the Hammersmith Apollo in October, the chosen male was gay *Big Brother* winner and *SM:TV* presenter Brian Dowling, who got slightly different treatment. According to concert-goers Alesha shouted, 'What are we going to do with this one, ladies?' before putting her high-heeled foot in his groin while the other two slapped him about. 'It was obvious that he loved every minute of it – and so did the girls,' said a fan. The show was a sell-out all over the country and the critics approved.

'Ashanti would have fainted at the sound of MC Alesha Dixon's quintuple-speed rhyming, and even Beyoncé might have struggled to match the power of Sabrina Washington's vocals,' said Lynsey Hanley of *The Daily Telegraph*. 'They worked the crowd individually and together, waving to the tweenies and taking impeccably democratic turns to sing. As ever, though, it was Dixon's sudden transformation from demure diva into growling ragga MC that provided the surprises.'

'It was difficult to believe this was Mis-Teeq's first UK tour,' said critic Robert Beaumont. 'The three girls established an immediate, and genuine, rapport with the crowd, while their band was tight and slick. It was refreshing to see such raw energy – and talent – in a world which is becoming increasingly dominated by image and packaging.'

In Manchester, on their fourth date, Sabrina told *Designer Magazine* that the girls were enjoying the tour so far. 'It's going really well,' she said. 'We've been waiting to do a tour for quite some time. We've been blessed by playing some of the rock festivals, which a lot of people wouldn't expect Mis-Teeq to do. When we did Glastonbury and V Festival we've gone down really well and the tents have been packed out, which is an amazing thing because Mis-Teeq are a band that kind of have mass appeal. I had this really old lady come up to me the other day [adopts posh voice] "I Love your song 'Scandalous', I think it's so fantastic."'

She also revealed that the three friends were truly beginning to revel in their new lives as pop stars and felt that the experience was enhanced because of the hard work that they had put in to getting there. 'Everything's been a highlight for us because we've worked really hard to get where we are. Our first album *Lickin' On Both Sides* going double platinum was a fantastic opportunity for us because before that people were saying urban music doesn't sell, but we proved them wrong. A lot of people were laughing on the other side of their faces after that. Also we've been blessed by having a second album *Eye Candy* that has done really well. I can't say anything has stood out more than any other.'

Alesha added that she was pleased that their talent hadn't been discovered on a reality show such as *Pop Idol* or *Popstars*, which had produced Girls Aloud and Hear'Say and made stars of Will Young, Gareth Gates and Alesha's future love rival Javine. She wouldn't want to have found stardom that way, she said. 'The reason being because of the stigma that comes with that. It's nothing to do with the talent or their vocal ability as artists. For us it's just that grounding of coming through the underground scene and working our way up slowly, I think we had a lot more respect. Therefore the media has worked for us because we're not putting ourselves up for criticism.'

The triumphant tour also left the girls feeling that yet another hurdle had been jumped. Now they were at the peak of their success, Alesha had not forgotten the nay-sayers she had faced at the bottom. 'There's always barriers that we're constantly trying to deal with,' she told *Designer Magazine*. 'When we first came out people used to say we'd never sell albums and then the album came out and it showed that a black urban act in the UK could sell records.'

But with late nights on stage, early-morning appearances on TV shows and interviews with local press, the girls were still missing out on their precious shut-eye. Not that they were complaining.

'We love being busy and we love performing,' said Alesha. 'Nothing comes close to that.'

'We knew it was going to be hard work when we started out on this – but I don't think anything can quite prepare you for how much hard work it is going to be, with all the travel and the lack of sleep,' Su-Elise told the *Liverpool Echo*. 'We might wake up a bit grumpy, but we are all girls together, and we are really girly – once we get there and start doing our hair and make-up and stuff, we're just like any other group of friends, we have a really good laugh together, and by the end of that, those smiles are genuine. This is the best job in the world, no matter how tough it can be, and we wouldn't change it for the world.'

As friends and admirers of Alesha Dixon will no doubt testify, when it comes to good causes, she has a heart of gold. For the philanthropic threesome the tour was too good a chance to miss, so they decided to use it to promote Cancer Research, pledging their support to a new campaign started by the charity which aimed to raise awareness of cancer among the young and ethnic communities in the run-up to a conference in early 2004. A plug for the charity was given in their tour brochure, free tickets were given for cancer-stricken youngsters and the group met young sufferers from around the country on their travels.

'We're really pleased to help support the work that Cancer Research UK is doing within the black community in trying to raise awareness of this disease, as cancer doesn't discriminate against race, age or colour,' said Alesha in the *Birmingham Post*.

The charity's director of communications, Susan Osborne, was convinced the group's involvement would help get the message across to young people in ethnic communities. 'Mis-Teeq's support is invaluable to us as we can get our messages out to younger and more diverse audiences, which will help prevent cancer for future generations and raise funds so we can continue our vital work.'

As well as the charity requests, the band were being inundated with endorsement offers and their increasingly high profile was beginning to swell the coffers. In September 2003, Barbie creators Mattel launched their Barbie Flavas range, with the blessing of the band. The new-look dolls moved away from the traditional blonde-haired, blue-eyed Barbies to better reflect the ethnic diversity of modern society. 'We're chuffed to bits to launch this range of dolls, because they're like us. They encourage girls – and boys – to express themselves,' said the girls.

'These dolls are all funky, modern and different,' said Su-Elise. 'They're a mixed bunch of various skin tones and hair colours. When we were growing up, kids always had blonde, blue-eyed Barbies.'

A more lucrative contract came when the girls were asked to put the R&B into Reebok. The sexy singers were reportedly paid a six-figure fee to follow in the footsteps of Jay Z and Samantha Mumba and promote the sportswear brand's new womenswear range. A newly kitted-out Sabrina confessed, 'We seem to spend half our time deciding who gets what rather than rehearsing and recording.'

Before embarking on the UK tour, Mis-Teeq were once again honoured in the MOBO nominations, in three categories, for UK Act of the Year and Best Single and Video for 'Scandalous'. This time there was no rivalry at home for Alesha as Harvey's So Solid Crew failed to get a mention. On the night, the girls blew the audience away with a brilliant set, complete with pyrotechnics, and a memorable performance of 'Scandalous' with rapper *du jour* Redman, who mixed his own track, 'Smash', with their biggest hit. They also set tongues wagging in the fashion world when they donned leather socks for the show.

'Redman – what an honour!' Alesha told *Designer Magazine* after the show. 'Great guy. "Smash" is a fantastic track and "Scandalous" just sat right on it. It couldn't have gone better if we tried and the chemistry on stage was brilliant.'

Su-Elise explained the much talked about footwear, 'We normally wear boots on stage, but we wore trainers that night because we really wanted to get grimy. Now everyone's going on about these leather socks we were wearing and it's like, what? . . . it's nice to know we're trendsetters!'

The fashion coup couldn't have come at a better time – just a month before the release of their next single, 'Style' – and it gave them plenty of opportunity to talk labels and shopping to their hearts' content. The track, released in November, which could have been a love song to Harvey, was about rejecting a sharp-dressed man for a 'man with a hip hop style' and proclaimed 'I need a rude boy, with some edge, I need a rough neck, making ends'.

'It's all about the kind of gear we find sexy on a man – I like a guy who knows how to put clothes together well,' explained Alesha to *Now* magazine. 'There's nothing more off putting than having to tell him what looks good and what's a big no-no!'

When it came to their own style, the thrifty threesome were still sticking to bigging up the high-street brands that they had worn before the big time, although the odd extravagance was clearly creeping in.

'We get our clothes at Topshop, places like that,' said Sabrina. 'You don't need designer clothes if you've got a style all of your own.' But she admitted to a passion for Alexander McQueen and added, 'We're all quite into fashion, which is why we enjoyed London Fashion Week so much. But I often mix and match, too, by combining designer clothes with high-street tags like Topshop.'

When it came to splashing the cash, however, it seemed love loosened Alesha's purse strings. 'Last year I spent £1,500 on a leather Prada jacket for my fiancé,' she confessed to the *Daily Star*. 'Sometimes I can be really careful about money and I don't like to spend that much.

'The most I've ever spent on an item of clothing for myself is a knee-length white dress from Versace, which cost £1,000. I guess the most outrageous thing I've worn is a long Voyage denim skirt with a white wolf printed on it. They asked me to wear it for the opening of their store, but I gave it back afterwards.'

She also revealed that the heavy make-up the girls wore for photo shoots and TV appearances was not up her street. 'I do like my high heels and we're experts at dancing in them now,' she told the *Sunday Mirror*. 'I don't like heavy, expensive make-up – Nivea cream, a bit of mascara and a nice lippy by Mac. 'We have to pile on the make-up for a photo shoot or TV studio, but as soon as we finish, we get in the car, get out our face wipes and take it off.'

In the midst of the tour to promote the new single the girls were whisked off to Japan where Alesha admitted to a fashion faux pas. During a live performance she wore her kimono back to front. 'I didn't know that wearing it in that way means "death" in Japan,' the mortified singer said. 'I think I offended most of Japan!'

There was added excitement on the trip, albeit of the wrong kind, when an earthquake struck Tokyo. The girls woke up to find the rooms of their swish hotel were shaking. 'It was awful,' revealed Alesha in *The Sun*. 'The whole hotel was shaking. We ran down to the lobby and all hell was breaking loose. People were panicking, not knowing where to go or what to do. I'd hate to go through something like that again.'

Thankfully, the girls escaped unscathed to continue their punishing schedule of gigs and promotion that stretched right through Christmas and the New Year. 'Style', however, failed to make the UK top ten, stalling at an unlucky 13, and it made no impact on the international charts either.

With their UK popularity seemingly on the wane, the new year brought a fresh onslaught on the Holy Grail of pop. Mis-Teeq was off to America.

CHAPTER SIX

Can't Get It Back

The New Year started with a pleasant surprise for Alesha, and her own little American victory, when one of the hottest producers in the States called her and asked her to star in his new video. Pharrell Williams was behind the biggest hits from Justin Timberlake and Britney Spears and also recorded as the frontman for N.E.R.D, along with Chad Hugo and Shay. Having spotted the stunning singer on the front of *Arena* magazine, Williams decided she was just the girl to dance in the promo for N.E.R.D's new single, 'She Wants To Move'. According to reports at the time, casting directors suggested supermodels, including Naomi Campbell, but Pharrell stuck to his guns and called the Brit beauty in the first week of January.

'I still can't believe this has happened. I got the call last Wednesday and on Thursday I was on a flight to LA,' Alesha told the *Daily Mirror*, on her return. 'Doing the video was a fantastic experience. My scenes were filmed in the desert and I had to ride around on the back of a motorbike. To get to see N.E.R.D at work was an amazing experience because in my opinion they are the hottest act in the world at the moment.'

The steamy video sees Alesha dancing on a podium wearing a silver fringed dress which bears an uncanny resemblance to the Latin outfits she would wear on *Strictly Come Dancing* three years later. The three band members watch her from a revolving stage and sing, 'She's sexy,' and the immortal line, 'Her ass is a spaceship I wanna ride.'

The same week, Mis-Teeq received the news that they had been nominated for two BRIT Awards, for Best British Urban Act and Best Single for 'Scandalous'. 'It's just amazing,' Alesha told the *Sunday Mirror*. 'We wrote "Scandalous" so long ago, it's like that song doesn't want to go away. It was just what we needed to hear before we kicked back into work again.'

Already, the group were busy working on a third album with songwriter Guy Chambers, who had previously penned numerous hits for Robbie Williams, including 'Angels', 'Millennium' and 'Let Me Entertain You'. 'At the moment it's sounding quite rocky but still very Mis-Teeq and very soulful,' revealed Alesha in the *Sunday Mirror*. 'Guy has brought out a different side to us, so we're going to take our time and make sure we get it right. Hopefully something will be out by the end of the year. We're so excited.'

With plans to spend a large chunk of the year in the States, wooing the tough American audience, it looked like it was going to be a good year for Mis-Teeq. 'I don't feel we've lost by travelling to America,' said Alesha after a few weeks promoting the band there. 'We've got nothing to lose. We're young and we've got ambition. If it doesn't happen, it wasn't meant to be.'

Asked about the future of the trio, Alesha was optimistic, revealing they had a five album deal with Telstar and were expecting to stay together long enough to fulfil it, but would 'take each day as it comes'. Her two hopes for 2004, she said, were 'a platinum-selling third album and success in America. Not out of the question I hope!'

After a romantic break in Dubai with Harvey, who had recently begun to rebuild his own career by winning the TV sports contest *The Games*, Alesha was back to work. Mis-Teeq booked time out to work in the States in April and May after throwing themselves into album number three.

Once again the long-awaited wedding to Harvey went on the backburner. 'We're trying to work it out,' said Alesha in February. 'Our lives are run by our diaries so we'll just have to figure it out – but it will happen. We're not worrying because there's no rush when we're going to be with each other for the rest of our lives. I will have a white wedding but I don't know if I'll get married in a church, I'm not sure.'

But before their American assault became a reality, the girls suffered a huge blow. In March, reports started to filter through about Telstar's financial troubles and the company went into administration in the first week of April with reported debts of around £8.5 million. The record label, which also had Craig David, The Cheeky Girls and The Hives on its books, had, according to tabloid reports, recently spent over a million in an unsuccessful attempt to relaunch Victoria Beckham's singing career. Telstar Executive Neil Palmer blamed a downturn in the music business, saying, 'This is a very sad day and unfortunately reflects the serious problems the industry as a whole is experiencing.'

'We are currently considering a number of ways forward, including the possibility of a realistic sale of the intellectual property and back catalogue of the business,' administrator Paul Stoneman said at the time. 'We have not discounted any options.'

With two hit albums to their name and a third underway, it seemed certain Mis-Teeq would be picked up by a different record label, and in April various offers were on the table. In a second blow, however, it was reported that the trio would lose thousands in royalties that Telstar owed them from sales of *Eye Candy*. Ironically, as the girls teetered on the brink of recognition in the States, they faced an uncertain future in their homeland.

As the legal issues continued to be ironed out, the band packed their bags and headed stateside for the summer. Their two-month stint in America was a big deal for Alesha, whose only childhood experience of travelling abroad was 'on a ferry with my family to France when I was five'.

A breakthrough came when they landed a deal with Reprise records, largely down to the backing of an influential patron, MTV presenter and chat show host Carson Daly. Daly had been on a recent holiday to France where he had heard 'Scandalous' played in bars and clubs – and he had fallen in love with it. On his return, he apparently persuaded the record company to release the track.

'We love Carson! Big up, Carson! He discovered us,' gushed Sabrina. 'He kind of heard the song and he went out that night to a club and he heard it again. Everyone was really getting down to it on the dance floor so he came back to the United States and he was like, "Who sings this song? It's called 'Scandalous', I don't know who sings it." But he kind of researched and found out it was us, and Bob's your uncle, Fanny's your aunt, and here we are!' She admitted that Mis-Teeq were as shocked as anyone to hear that the US radio stations had picked up the track. 'We were told the song was being played on the radio and we were like, yeah, right,' she says. 'It was only when I got to New York and heard "Scandalous" being played in a shop that I realized it really was. It's pretty amazing.'

And with phrases like 'Bob's your uncle, Fanny's your aunt' it was clear the Brit babes had no intention of losing their London street cred while vying for American adoration. 'They love the English accent,' she told *The Guardian*. 'They're kind of amazed when we sing. We don't sound American – our sound is very, very British. We're not going to go out to America and try and imitate what Americans do, because they do it the best. Originality is definitely the key, we want to keep sounding as British as we can.'

Released in May, 'Scandalous' reached number 35 in the Hot 100 charts, number 11 in the Billboard Top 40 Mainstream chart and number four in the Hot Dance Singles chart, making it their biggest US hit. In July, the release of *Catwoman*, with 'Scandalous' as its theme tune, boosted their profile even more. The choice of the track for the Halle Berry blockbuster over Britney Spears' 'Outrageous' meant the girls were invited to the LA premiere, which they attended with their new champion Carson Daly.

The movie coincided with the release of their eponymous US album, *Mis-Teeq*. A blend of the best bits from their two UK albums, including all seven hit singles, the album got a disappointing reception. One reviewer called the songs 'harmlessly vacuous, powered by infectious grooves, sassy attitude and the heavy branding of satisfying, if vaguely familiar, choruses,' and went on, 'In a game of style over substance, the act prevails. From an American point of view, however, Mis-Teeq's wild British success is a mystery.' *Mis-Teeq* reached just 125 in the charts.

Having rarely strayed far from Hertfordshire and London, Alesha did occasionally find her new experiences as frightening as they were exciting. One particular concert had the girls quaking in their trademark boots.

'It was a gig in Chicago,' she later recalled. 'All the other acts on the bill were hardcore gangster hip hop rappers, they were all really swearing and the crowd loved it. There we were, in our little girly dresses waiting to go on and sing "Scandalous". We were so scared. Sabrina said, "Alesha, just do your rapping and swear your head off." We changed into our jeans and the crowd were OK in the end. I have no idea how we got booked as we didn't fit in at all.'

Despite their misfortune on both sides of the pond, however, the girls stuck together while they pondered their future. Firm friends, they had been through a lot together, enjoyed each other's company and clearly didn't want the dream to end just yet. They may have been together 24/7 but, according to Alesha, there were no arguments. 'We tend to have more adult debates,' she laughed. 'We're three strong-minded women but we see that as an asset. If we didn't like each other, we wouldn't be doing it.'

Having spent most of the summer apart, Harvey and Alesha were keen to confirm their commitment to each other and, in September, they finally named the big day. They would tie the knot on 19 June 2005, they announced, and Harvey's long-term friend, Spurs star Sean Davis, would be Best Man. Despite her unconventional upbringing, the sanctity of marriage was important to Alesha and she had her heart set on a traditional white wedding with all the trimmings.

'I'm an old-fashioned girl at heart,' she told the *Daily Mirror*. 'I just want our wedding to be simple and lovely. I'm really excited. I'm going to have a soul choir sing as I walk down the aisle, and my sister and my best friend will be my bridesmaids.'

While Alesha toured America, the tough So Solid MC, being somewhat overshadowed by his fiancée's success, was left holding the duster! Busy working on new material and attempting to launch a career as an actor and TV presenter, Harvey confessed he was becoming quite the homemaker.

'I do the housework when she's jet-setting in America,' he told the *Daily Record*. 'We've moved on to the next level. There's been a lot of growing up to do. I still go out, but it's only once a week now.'

The busy star did manage to find time to help Harvey out on his new single, 'Natural High', which featured her distinctive tones. The duet, slated for release in January 2005, was another stab at resurrecting Harvey's solo career, and the So Solid rapper revealed that Alesha had already helped out on his previous songs, helping to write the choruses, but that he had banned her from singing on them.

'Alesha writes most of my songs' hooks,' he confessed. 'I just don't let her sing them. I always get someone else. But we do like to keep it in the family, however. She's on my single this time round, but she won't be in the video. We want to keep it away from 'Harvey and Alesha'. We are not into the Posh and Becks thing. She's a star in her own right and so am I.'

Harvey had already had some presenting work on T4, taken part in a football reality show called *The Match* and had kicked off his acting career with a small part in the Steven Seagal movie, *Out For a Kill*. 'When I made the film with Steven Seagal I had an interesting time. He taught me a lot and he even took me to dinner with Quentin Tarantino,' he said. 'That was amazing, but I'd much rather be a success in Britain — if it happens in America, it happens.'

In October, he unveiled plans to become a model and said he had signed up with a model agency. 'I'm prepared to go all the way with modelling, but I don't mean I'll go naked – my lunchbox is only for one woman,' he laughed. 'The only way I'd strip off is for charity, but anything else would be selling your soul. I don't see myself as a model, it's just a job. I am a brand now, just like my idol Will Smith. I sing, present, act and model too.'

Alesha, meanwhile, was still focusing on her music career, in spite of a flurry of movie offers, the likes of which Harvey could only dream. 'We've read scripts but nothing's taken our fancy,' she revealed in the *Sunday Mirror*. 'It's not a priority but it would be brilliant to do something together. Something more *Charlie's Angels*-style than *Spice World*.'

Sadly *Mis-Teeq: The Movie* was never to be. The second US release, 'One Night Stand', failed to make a huge impact, missing out on the top 40 and peaking at number 8 in the Hot Dance Singles chart.

Christmas 2004 was a time to reunite with their families, reflect on the future and give themselves space for some serious soul-searching. With no record deal in place in the UK, the girls sat down for a long heart-to-heart and eventually decided that, after eight great years together, it was time to go their separate ways. The band announced their split in January 2005.

'They've done it so they can explore other opportunities,' the group's spokesman stated. 'But the band loved their time together and they'll remain friends.'

Their swan-song, for pigeon movie *Valiant*, was a brilliant cover of the Andrews Sisters' wartime classic 'Shoo Shoo Baby'. They followed this with a greatest hits album, released in April, which reached number 28 in the album charts. But having been so close to her bandmates for so long, Alesha found adjusting to the split trying at first. 'I keep expecting there to be three of us,' she admitted. 'It's a bit lonely — I look to my side and they're not there any more.'

As Alesha began thinking about a solo career, the Mis-Teeq members remained firm friends. Unlike many band break-ups, there were no bitter recriminations and no backstabbing. Everything appeared to be perfectly amicable.

'There wasn't a massive bust-up,' confirmed Alesha. 'There's this myth that girl groups are all really bitchy and hate each other, but we weren't forced to sing together. We were friends. We split because we had no contractual ties, and we thought it was the right thing to do: go out on a high.'

Even so, she admitted it was a tough decision, but that the lack of a label in the UK had promoted the split. 'It was really frustrating. We were sounding better than we'd ever sounded, looking better than we'd ever looked and it all felt like it was going on to the next level. We came back to Britain and made a decision. Do we shop around for a new home and start from scratch somewhere else or do we call it a day?'

Sabrina took a break from music to experiment with different styles, while Su-Elise, who had interrupted her business studies degree to join the band, went back to college to train as a teacher. She eventually opened her own stage and dance school in Gravesend, Kent.

Over a year later, asked in a web chat whether she would work again with the girls or think about releasing the unused material from the third album, Alesha said she would be giving away the music they had written. 'The material from the third album I'd like to give to other artists to be honest,' she replied.

'But I'd never say never about a collaboration. There's still love there and the girls are cool, so who knows? But I don't know if people are bored of bands coming back together.'

The split left Alesha with time to sit back and relax for the first time in years. While she is naturally hard-working and energetic, her enforced vacation made Alesha focus on song-writing and, of course, on those all-consuming wedding plans.

Looking back on Mis-Teeq, she began to realize what an exhausting three years the band's success had brought her. As usual, she wasn't complaining. 'I'd feel terrible to not stop and soak it all up and take it all in and really enjoy it,' she said later. 'So every single day when I go to work, I'm happy to go to work. The worst there'll be is just lack of sleep, but that's natural. The human body can only run on so much energy before it gets tired. But I enjoy every single day, I really do. Don't get me wrong, it was a whirlwind, but I took it all in. I documented it the whole way, I took photos all the time and my camcorder everywhere, and my mum's got twenty-odd scrap books of everything we did, video tapes . . . so I've got it all documented. I've got a lot of memories.'

CHAPTER SEVEN

Love and Lipstick

Growing up in Hertfordshire, Alesha, like most girls, dreamed of finding the right guy and having a big white wedding in a beautiful setting. In June 2005, her dream was set to come true in the five-star splendour of Brocket Hall, a lavish stately home which the Alesha of her childhood could only fantasize about. Set in 543 acres just outside Welwyn Garden City, the stunning 300-year-old red-brick mansion, which was once the home of Prime Minister Lord Melbourne, overlooks Broadwater Lake and two golf courses. The creamy yellow walls of the sumptuous ballroom, where wedding breakfasts are served, are hung with original oil paintings, whose subjects gaze down upon the long antique table and the crystal chandeliers that hang from the decorative vaulted ceiling.

The guest bedrooms are beautifully decorated and the bridal suite boasts a four-poster bed, antique furniture and stunning views over the lake and architect James Paine's eighteenth-century Palladian bridge. It was a far cry from the Battersea streets that Harvey roamed as a child, and a huge leap from the tiny terrace just a few miles away that had been Alesha's home.

As the singer busied herself with plans for the big day, she also had a new solo career to look forward to. In April, just over two months after Mis-Teeq split, she landed a deal with Polydor, reported to be worth around £500,000 and began working on new material straight away.

But a dark cloud passed over the singer's fairytale ending in the months before her wedding, when Harvey was summoned to court to answer a charge of assaulting a police officer. The rapper had attacked the policeman after being stopped for using a mobile phone while driving, after a trip to Alesha's home in Welwyn Garden City in January. The officer was reported to have been forced to use CS gas in self-defence, and on 31 May, Harvey was found guilty. Less than a month before their wedding, the couple faced the possibility that Harvey could be sent to jail, but after a nerve-racking week, he was instead sentenced to 150 hours' community service and was anxious to show his remorse. 'I will get on with my community punishment and get back to reality,' he said. 'I have learned my lesson and it is a bad example to kids. You live and learn.'

With a week to go, bride and groom disappeared on their respective bachelor parties. In typically diverse style, Harvey chose a raving weekend in club capital Ibiza with thirteen mates, where they partied until the early hours of the morning, while Alesha opted for a quieter Spanish venue, taking a few close friends for a weekend in Marbella.

On 19 June 2005, a blushing bride prepared for her big day at one of the most beautiful manor houses in the country. While Harvey had confessed to last-minute butterflies the week before, Alesha wouldn't have suffered many qualms on the day, knowing that what she felt for Harvey was 'unconditional love'. Her family background, she later admitted, meant she was determined to have a stable, solid marriage from that day forth. 'My parents never married, but I wanted a husband,' she told the *Daily Mail* in 2009.

As she walked down the aisle, Alesha looked stunning in a two-piece strapless Kosibah dress in white satin, with a fishtail skirt that featured panels in a deep red. The bustline was decorated with embroidery swirls in the same red and Swarovski crystals, and her two bridesmaids, her best friend and her sister Leyanne, wore matching claret strapless dresses. Alesha, who had designed the wedding dress herself, along with the team from Kosibah, made a lasting impression on her waiting groom. 'When I saw her walking down the aisle I was gone,' Harvey told the *Daily Mail* later. 'I cried my eyes out and my Best Man, Sean Davis, was crying too.'

The wedding breakfast was cooked by friend and celebrity chef Jean-Christophe Novelli, and along with the couple's sizeable families, guests included MC Romeo, Lisa Maffia and Alesha's former Mis-Teeq bandmates, Sabrina Washington and Su-Elise Nash. Watched by mum Beverley and her beloved grandmothers, Alesha tied the knot with the man she wanted to spend the rest of her life with. It was, simply, the happiest day of her life.

The singer settled into married life in the couple's new Hertfordshire home and they seemed the perfect match. A keen footballer who played for AFC Wimbledon on Saturdays, Harvey had found a fellow footie nut in his new wife, who liked nothing more than snuggling up in front of *Match of the Day*.

'It's great to sit back and watch the matches together,' she said in a *Sun* interview, but admitted that when their two teams met the potential for a clash was always there. 'I'm a Gooner and Harvey is a Liverpool fan. It's war in our house when we play each other.'

Obsessively tidy Alesha's pals call her Monica after the house-proud Courteney Cox character in her favourite show, *Friends*. Harvey, it seemed, shared her love of housework. In fact, Alesha revealed on *Soccer AM* that he calmed his nerves before a Saturday match by vacuuming the house.

'Some people say it feels no different when you marry, but it does. It's more settled and relaxed,' revealed Alesha, two months into their marriage. 'We want to build a life together. There's no point in arguing about stupid things. Don't get me wrong, it's not perfect, but because we love each other, we want to work at it.'

Over the course of the relationship, late nights were replaced with cosy nights in, and even the couple's musical tastes changed. 'It used to be nightclubs till 3am; now it's Sunday roasts at my local pub. I think that probably reflects the music I listen to. Guitars! Five years ago I couldn't have imagined listening to The Zutons or Razorlight. Now I love them,' said Alesha in *The Times*.

As with all brides, no sooner had the ink on the marriage certificate dried than the questions about starting a family began. Alesha was in no doubt that she would love to have children in the future but, at just twenty-six, she felt she had other things to achieve first. 'I'd love to start a family, but when I have children, that'll be my main priority,' she declared in the *News of the World*. 'I'm starting my own venture and I want to be selfish for a little bit longer. And I couldn't be happier!'

In another interview she was waiting for the time to be right. 'I don't think you can put an age on having a baby. It'll be when I feel ready, which could be soon, but who knows? I'd never put off having a baby because of the job I do. I really want a little girl, not a boy because boys are mean!'

Influenced by her own experiences as a child, Alesha was determined that her own babies would be brought up in a stable environment. 'I believe if a child is in a secure, stable environment they can go out into the world fearless,' she said. 'But if a child doesn't have that feeling of security because of the uncertainties around them, it affects them. Probably some of the greatest songwriters in the world are insecure people because they have inner fears.'

In the meantime, the newlyweds had plenty to keep them occupied and everything looked rosy in the Harvey household. Alesha was working with Johnny Douglas, Paul Epworth and Girls Aloud songwriter Brian Higgins on tracks for her debut solo album, and Harvey was presenting on T4 and had been asked to return to Sky One's celebrity footballing programme *The Match*, after gaining automatic entry having impressed with his ball skills the previous year. During training in October, he would be leaving the marital home to share a house with Dane Bowers, Jonathan Wilkes, Andy Scott-Lee, ex-*Corrie* star Danny Young and *The X Factor*'s Steve Brookstein.

To Alesha's amusement, Harvey decided to dye his hair red for the series. 'Last year, I did a blond streak,' he said. 'I'm just a nutter. I'm like Rooney, I do lose it on the pitch sometimes. Once the eyebrows join up, I'm in the zone. I love battling people. It's all part of the sport. But after the final whistle, it's all about having a drink in the bar. I love it. Doing the show last year was one of the best experiences of my life. I've never played in front of 60,000 people before. It was amazing.'

And he revealed that his new wife would be yelling from the sidelines. 'My lovely wife is a football fanatic. Ian Wright was her hero until she saw me and Ian having a big argument on the pitch last year.'

In August 2006, Harvey started rehearsals for his first ever West End show, *Daddy Cool,* which was based on the songs of Boney M and also starred *Popstars: The Rivals* runner-up Javine Hylton. At the same time, after a year enjoying marital bliss and working on the new album, Alesha launched her solo career with the single 'Lipstick' and an announcement that she never wanted to rest again. 'I had a year of relaxing and that's enough,' she laughed. 'I never want to relax again. I've got too much pent-up energy.'

The song, which she performed on the last live *Top of the Pops* in July, was a raunchy anthem to sisterhood, urging women to get together and not let men come between them. 'Why do you think that every girl out there's your enemy?' sang Alesha. The vocals owed more to the Spice Girls than to Destiny's Child, and the growling raps had disappeared from the sound to leave a more mellow sing-speak style. Alesha confessed she wanted to put her days as an MC behind her. 'My veins used to pop out of my neck when I did that stuff,' she told *The Observer Magazine*. 'I can't watch it now. I cringe. But at the time it felt right. I didn't MC, I shouted. But I was very passionate about it.'

The video saw Alesha dancing in a super-short mini and dragging a lipstick along the wall before breaking it and writhing around in a skintight red bodice. In interviews to promote the single, Alesha urged women to stop being mean about each other.

'I do care about the way women address each other. I think it's really ugly how women can be quite jealous of each other,' she explained to the *I Like Music* website. 'If a woman walks in the room, and not all women do it, but I've clocked some women doing it, and they kind of start at your feet and work their way up and really scan you and it's like checking out the competition. But why do we see each other as competition? All for the attention of men, it's just silly, at different levels and different examples of it. I just think it's a nicer trait to have to support each other. I like myself more when I'm happy for people. I don't wish bad on people. I just think girls should be taking it easier on each other and stop blaming each other for everything.'

The down-to-earth diva voiced her frustration at celebrity magazines that specialized in bitching about women. 'I don't like it when women look in magazines and get pleasure out of seeing people looking bad and things like that. Why do you do that? But do you know why they do it? It's to make themselves feel better, and that goes back to that whole security thing. If you're comfortable in your own skin then you can be comfortable and happy for other people, and I think that's where it needs to start from really.'

The lyrics for the track, produced by Swedish producer Anders Bagge, were written in a hotel room in one evening, and Alesha was so thrilled with her efforts that she phoned her mum there and then and sang the chorus down the line. 'The subject matter was like a spark, it just came to me in that moment, it just flowed.'

As in the past, with Mis-Teeq, there was more than one version of the song, with one remix featuring MC Shystie delivering the kind of rap Alesha herself might have added in her MC-ing days. 'I wanted to work with Shystie, because a) she's female and b) she's a great MC and I've just done a radio tour going to all pirate radio and specialist urban stations to show them that, OK, so my single is quite rock and pop, but in actual fact, I'm still doing my remixes, I've still got my R&B remix, I've just got an Agent X garage "Four to the Floor" remix done as well, because that's the music I used to love and I'm putting that on vinyl too for the DJs, because it's in my blood, I have to do it. I have to go and visit the pirate radio stations and I have to show these people that got me there in the first place that I still care about them and I owe them a lot.'

Harking back to her roots, and growing up in a white area as a mixed race child, Alesha said she wanted to set an example to youngsters in ethnic communities. 'I remember seeing Neneh Cherry on the TV when I was little and turning to my mum and saying, "Mummy, she looks just like me." I want to do that for black and mixed-race kids now. There aren't a lot of us out there.'

But she admitted that the thought of reinventing and relaunching herself was making her nervous. 'Of course there are nerves,' she told *The Observer Magazine*. 'Of course, I know the music business can be full of nutters. And of course I'm aware that the hit rate of black British female solo artists isn't great. But I believe one hundred per cent in the music. I wanted to make a pop album that I loved. And I've done it.'

As the single hit the shops she confessed to a fan in a web chat that she was anxious about the single's potential performance. 'I woke up this morning and actually felt quite sick. I'm feeling really nervous. It's a horrible feeling, you can't really gauge how it's doing. It's really scary. I just pray that tomorrow I get some good news, but on my break today I'm going to buy my own single!'

In fact, there was good news on the way when, despite her first solo single having been in the shops for just two days, she received a MOBO nomination for Best UK Female, along with Beverley Knight, Corinne Bailey Rae, Jamelia and Keisha White.

During interviews for the single Alesha revealed that she'd once been chatted up by Prince Harry in a nightclub. 'It was flattering,' she told the *News of the World*. 'I was dancing with friends in London club Pangaea when a guy came up to me and said, "Prince Harry would like to meet you."

'I told Harry I'd loved singing at the Palace for the Queen's Jubilee. He asked me if I wanted a drink. I declined, but said, "Can I have a sip of yours?" He said, "Go on then!" Afterwards I didn't know if I should have done that!

'I didn't fancy him. He's just a little boy to me, although he is handsome.' But she added that hubby Harvey, who had recently been chatted up by Halle Berry, was not the jealous type. 'Harvey's in the industry, so he understands,' she said. 'When you're secure in your relationship, you can take it all with a pinch of salt. Otherwise jealousy will eat you up.'

'Lipstick' was not the huge success that Alesha had hoped for, peaking at number 14 in the charts. But Alesha was still looking forward to the release of her album, *Fired Up*, in October and her second single, 'Knockdown'. The breezy ragga-style pop song was about picking yourself up from the knocks that life deals you, and the video showed Alesha in a variety of outfits and vaguely comical hats singing, 'Ha, ha, ha, ha, ha, ho, ho, ho, ho, ho.'

'It is about life's lows, but I don't want to write depressing songs,' she explained. 'The world's bad enough without my music depressing anyone. I'm performing to uplift the crowd and get people motivated.'

As she sang to make the world happy, Alesha was about to learn how to deal with her own 'Knockdown'.

CHAPTER EIGHT

Scandalous

To her contemporaries in Welwyn Garden City, Alesha was, by 2006, the girl who had it all. She had shaken off her poverty-stricken background, forged a hugely successful music career with a girl group, and was enjoying her first run at a solo career. She was beautiful, rich and happily married to the man she adored. Harvey was busily carving out a career as an actor, and enjoying his West End role in the Boney M musical *Daddy Cool*. Alesha had just finished recording her first solo album and was launching her first single.

Then, as winter approached, the dream became a nightmare as the two things she valued most in life – her marriage and her music career – dramatically collapsed.

After the disappointing performance of 'Lipstick', her second single failed to make any impact on the top 40, stalling at number 45. In October, just a fortnight before the release of *Fired Up*, her record label, Polydor, dropped a bombshell. Due to poor sales, they were cancelling her contract and would not be releasing the album after all.

As a shocked Alesha took stock of her career and wondered which path to take next, she leant on her husband for support. After all, he had suffered a similar fate at the hands of his record company, but had picked himself up and reinvented himself as an actor. Then she was dealt the cruellest blow of all. Two weeks after her solo career was axed, Harvey's affair with *Daddy Cool* co-star

Javine Hylton became the subject of lurid press reports, which claimed he had been caught in his lover's bed by her long-term boyfriend, Karl Gordon. The tabloids alleged that the furious record producer had then phoned Alesha and spilled the beans before her husband had a chance to break it to her himself.

In an interview shortly afterwards, Harvey – real name Mike Harvey – denied this version of events and said that he had told Alesha about the affair himself. 'I had an affair and had to tell Alesha about it inside our four walls,' he said. 'The reports that said Javine's boyfriend came in and that we were rolling around the house were classic. The story was one hundred per cent rubbish. I had to tell Alesha myself and suffer the repercussions. It was not easy to do that, as you can imagine – not easy to tell your wife you had an affair.'

In another article, in December 2007, Javine admitted that Karl did find Harvey at her house, but in more innocent circumstances. 'We were not caught in bed, romping,' she told the *Daily Mirror*. 'We weren't swinging from chandeliers. My boyfriend didn't walk in and see us naked on top of each other. One morning, Karl decided to come to the house. He walked in, saw Harvey, who had been staying in the spare room, and that was it. There was no fighting, no confrontation. Then Karl called Alesha and told her.'

According to the former *Popstars: The Rivals* contestant, Javine then faced a tough forty-eight hours as Harvey went home to sort things out with his wife of just a year. 'I told Harvey that he didn't have to leave Alesha,' she insists. 'As much as I loved him I had no right to ask him to leave his wife.'

After tense and heart-breaking discussions, Alesha and Harvey split for good and the rapper moved in with Javine.

'The irony is, I embarked on them [her solo career and marriage] both at the same time, then lost them both in the same month,' Alesha recalled two years later in *The Guardian*. 'I'm sitting here smiling today, though. At the time, you can't help thinking, "What have I done?" Because I tried to be a professional, I tried to treat people respectfully, I was a good wife, so what have I done? I believe you reap what you sow, so in my gut, I can't help feeling like something was trying to be flushed out of my life.

'I worked hard, I put my heart and soul into it, I've got a good mental attitude and my life was pulled out from underneath me. I didn't know where to step. I was just lost. Within two weeks it felt like the world had collapsed on my head.'

With Christmas fast approaching, and reeling from her double blow, the devastated singer packed her husband's clothes into a black bin bag and tried to hide from the public gaze.

'Christmas that year was quite a dark time,' she said. 'Anyone who knows me knows that my music career and marriage were the most important things. And I lost them within two weeks of each other. I believe in karma – and I sat there thinking, "I must have done something." It was a really weird time, a time where I had to force myself to believe all these things were being swept away for a reason. Believe me, it wasn't easy.'

And as if dealing with losing the love of her life wasn't enough, the public gaze had turned its spotlight onto her private life in a way she'd never had to deal with before. Suddenly, Harvey and Javine were all over the papers and Alesha's every move was reported. Her first night out after the split, when she attended a Take That gig and aftershow party, made headlines, and Alesha found the whole thing humiliating.

'It was so important to me to be a role model – to be married with strong foundations. I found it very embarrassing. I hibernated. I didn't even want to go to my local shop because everyone knew I'd been in this solid relationship for six years. Oh God, it was horrible,' she told the *People*.

As always in times of trouble, Alesha turned to her family for support. Beverley rushed to her side the moment Alesha told her of Harvey's betrayal, and grandmothers Clem and Maureen rallied round to help out their beloved granddaughter. Surrounded by close friends and family the battered star began to recover with dignity and characteristic determination.

'I refuse to be depressed. It's just a waste of time,' she explained in *The Sun*. 'By the time new year came round I was already feeling better. I'm very good at talking myself out of feeling down. I'm good at healing quickly. Plus, I didn't feel I was the victim, even though it was portrayed like that. My morals never changed, I'm a good person and I was a good wife. I shouldn't hold my head in shame. Why should I be miserable?'

Another positive was a renewed bond with her dad, who was living in Thailand at the time. 'As you get older you realize that your parents are human beings – not superheroes – and they're allowed to make mistakes,' she said in 2009. 'As a child, though, you're selfish, just thinking about your needs. Dad was always a part of my life. And we became a lot closer after what happened between me and Harvey.'

A new year and a new start, and Alesha was keen to get her life back once more. 'I'd been sitting on my couch and I was down all the time,' she recalled later in an interview with *The Sun*. 'But one evening a lightbulb went off in my head and the next morning I started making calls, starting to make things happen. I had to start the engine myself. For my own sanity and peace of mind, I had to be positive. So many women have told me, "I would have spent months and months being depressed." But I just refused to.

'My mum always taught me that no matter what you go through, there are people going through much worse. And I realized that what I had outweighed what I had lost. I had my friends and family. My close friends were with me all the time. You realize what's important in life.'

Her first move was to redecorate the home she had shared with Harvey, in an attempt to erase all memories of him.

'She did everything to get rid of any memories,' recalled Harvey later. 'One day I came back and she had renovated the house. All my stuff was in bin liners. She even took my So Solid platinum disc down.'

Next, in February 2007, she decided to rid herself of the one thing left from the glitzy day that should have been the happiest of her life – she put her wedding dress up for auction on eBay. The stunning ivory Kosibah gown with the red embroidery was designed by the singer herself but Alesha could no longer stand it being in the house. With a reserve price of £2,000, and including the veil she had worn eighteen months before, it was to go to the highest bidder, with all proceeds going to charity. With it she released a statement that read, 'I've decided to sell this beautiful one-off dress which I designed myself ... It would be a shame for it to go to waste! ... Good luck and I hope you enjoy. Lots of love, Alesha.'

The public message to Harvey was clear. Alesha was showing the world she was over him and well on the way to recovery. Even Harvey had to admit that it hurt.

With the future stars of show business and principal Warren Bacci of Top Hat Stage School at Alesha's former school Monk's Walk, in Welwyn Garden City.

Cheers: Alesha and her mum Beverley, with whom she shares a close relationship.

Sister act: Alesha clutching her Capital FM Award with sister Leyanne in 2004.

Rocking the red carpet with her goddaughter at the premiere of *High School Musical – Live On Stage*.

Puppy love: Alesha and Daisy, with whom she fell head-over-heels at the Southridge RSPCA Animal Centre.

An animal lover, Alesha poses for the 2008 PDSA calendar with her dog Roxy.

Mis-Teeq at the MOBO Awards in 2001, the year they released their debut album.

Su-Elise Nash, Sabrina Washington and Alesha at the BRIT Awards in 2002 where they performed and received a nomination for Best British Newcomer.

All smiles (almost): the girl band pose with Dr Fox and Simon Cowell at the Woman of the Year Awards 2002, where they scooped the Best Band award.

What a year: collecting their award for Best Garage Act at the 2002 MOBO Awards.

Alesha dazzles the crowds with LL Cool J, with whom she presented the Awards.

The girls collected the R&B/Soul Award on behalf of the late songstress Aaliyah in 2002, whose act inspired their success.

The success of their first album propelled Mis-Teeq into the limelight. Here they perform on *Later with Jools Holland* in 2002.

Hitting a treble: game playing on the *Top of the Pops* Saturday show in 2003.

Centre stage: Alesha delights fans at Party in the Park in 2003.

So Solid: Alesha with her then boyfriend MC Harvey in 2002.

In happier times: the couple perform together at T4 Pop Beach 2003.

With Jade Goody and Joanne Beckham at the wedding of mutual friends in 2005, the same year Alesha and MC tied the knot.

Unaware of a budding romance between her husband and his co-star, Alesha attends the opening of the musical *Daddy Cool* in 2006.

A friend in need: fellow musician Jamelia (left) was always very supportive of Alesha.

Alesha was devastated when she discovered her husband was having an affair with her friend Javine (right).

'I was gutted when she sold the dress,' he said at the *Fantastic Four* premiere that June. 'It was heartbreaking because it was a huge part of our special day and it caught me by surprise. I have to deal with it.'

The repentant rapper also admitted he felt terrible about the hurt he had caused his ex-wife, saying that he simply fell in love with Javine. 'The way I went about it was wrong – I know that and am owning up. The honest truth is that I had an affair. People fall out of love with someone and they move on. It's not a crime, it's how you go about it.'

And he admitted that Alesha's dignified handling of the affair meant she would always mean a lot to him. 'I'm in love with Javine but I love Alesha for the woman she was and is. I wish I had done things a better way rather than having an affair.'

As Harvey was no doubt unaware, reports that the wedding dress had sold for a whopping £7,500 were slightly off the mark. In fact the highest bid turned out to be a false one and the beautiful gown stayed with Alesha 'I didn't even sell it in the end!' she told *The Observer*. 'I put it up there and some-one put up a false bid so I've still got the bloody thing, unfortunately.'

By the spring, Alesha was ready to take the advice she doled out to others in her ill-fated single, 'Knockdown': 'Ya soul's feeling shot down, lucks out, but ya gotta carry on'. It's a philosophy that pulled her through on the darkest of days.

'It felt like the ground had been moved from beneath my feet,' she revealed in the *Daily Mirror*. 'I felt at a complete loss because the two most important things in my life had gone. But when you are knocked down you have two choices – stay down or get back up, stronger. I think all human beings can surprise themselves when they are in situations where they are tested. That's when you see your true character coming out and I was definitely tested. I'd never wish it on myself, but I'm kind of glad it happened.'

It was time to pick herself up and look at where she would go next. She had not given up on her hopes of forging a successful music career and had plenty of song-writing ideas up her sleeve. As all artists know, real heartbreak is a great inspiration when it comes to putting pen to paper.

'I never lost the desire to carry on in music – that's all I know, all I've ever dreamed of doing, it's all I've ever wanted to do so, I think, never give up,' said the determined diva. To broaden her horizons, however, she also signed up to star in a movie, *Milestones,* with Brian Cox and Alex Kingston. Set in the London jazz scene, it centres on an ageing musician who takes a young and talented prodigy under his wing.

As Alesha pondered her choices, out of the blue came two phonecalls which were about to change her life. First on the line was Brian Higgins of song-writing team Xenomania, who had worked with Alesha on the previous album and who was behind all twenty of Girls Aloud's hits, as well as singles for the Sugababes, the Pet Shop Boys and many more. Brian said he was keen to write songs with Alesha, despite the record company's decision to ditch her solo album.

The next call would give her a chance to climb to the next level: from struggling singer to national superstar.

'Brian Higgins of Xenomania called me up out of the blue and said he wanted to write with me, even though there was no record company there,' she said. 'And then *Strictly* happened. From the moment I met [dance partner] Matthew Cutler and we went into training, I was just converted. Every day I was just smiling and having fun. I laughed a lot for four months.'

As she prepared to relaunch herself, however, Alesha suffered new heartache in July when it was announced that Javine was pregnant with Harvey's baby. Having discussed future plans and starting a family with Harvey, the news must have come as a bitter blow to the now single twenty-nine-year-old. She admitted later that she worried that she may never have the opportunity to have a family of her own.

'When I look back to two years ago, there were so many things that scared me: the uncertainty of my career, the failure of my marriage,' she revealed in the *Daily Mail* in 2008. 'I used to wonder what was going to happen to my dream of having a family. At the time, it was devastating but actually it was the turning point for me.'

As well as getting back to work on her music, *Strictly Come Dancing* was exactly the tonic she needed. Being determined, energetic and naturally elegant, Alesha was ideal for the show and the famously gruelling training schedule – which can mean dancing for forty hours a week and can prove exhausting for even the fittest of sportsmen and women – was guaranteed to take her mind off her messy personal problems. For a girl who admitted, 'I have a problem with having days off, even as a child,' it was better than therapy. Fate had intervened in Alesha's life in the best possible way.

In hindsight, the show was the greatest thing that could have happened at that point, but she admits that she had doubts about taking it on, fearing for her credibility. 'I didn't say yes straight away,' she revealed. 'When I was in Mis-Teeq I said I'd never do a reality show. Or if I did, the only one would be *Strictly*. In the music industry there is a certain amount of snobbery – and *Strictly* was a risk for me. I didn't want people thinking I was using it as a vehicle. But I finally thought, "Who cares what people think? I know why I'm doing it."'

As the wounded warbler began to heal, she found forgiveness for her ex-husband. 'Everybody makes mistakes,' she said, magnanimously in an interview with the *People*. 'But if someone shows they are sorry – and they regret their actions – then that's all you need to move forward. It takes a bigger person to forgive than to hold a grudge. It's all about how you recover from a bad situation, what you do afterwards and how you move forward.'

'I have let go of my negative energy towards him. If you're angry, bitter or stressed you just end up making yourself ill. So I had to let it go for my own peace of mind.'

CHAPTER NINE

Strictly Stunning

For holidaymakers in Britain, the summer of 2007 was a washout, being the wettest in England and Wales since records began. For Alesha, the downpours were over and the blue skies were returning. And with her newly packed schedule, the weather outside was irrelevant as she was either in the recording studio or training daily with dance partner Matthew Cutler.

A sense of rhythm and an innate elegance is only half the battle in *Strictly*. The other half is pure hard work and dedication, and Latin American champ Matthew must have known he'd hit the jackpot with his new dance partner. Not only is she passionate about dancing but she pushes herself to the absolute limit and won't rest until she's happy with what she's achieved.

'When we met I could tell straight away that she was confident and had lots of energy. I was very happy!' Matthew said. And before they had even danced together on the programme, he was convinced Alesha could go all the way to the final. 'In my career I've won practically every category I've been in,' he said during training. 'The only title that eludes me is the *Strictly Come Dancing* trophy. This year with Alesha is definitely my best shot. Alesha is a massive bundle of energy, my problem will be to try and channel it in the right way.' In fact, over the course of series five of *Strictly Come Dancing*, the couple would put in a record 401 training hours. Alesha loved the fact that she was getting fit in the process.

'Before I became a musician I was very sporty, and ever since I have wanted to get back to a good level of fitness,' she said. Another reason for taking part was the chance to receive the dance tuition she craved as a child and had to live without. 'I've always wondered how far I could have gone with it if I could have carried on, and how far I could have pushed myself. I thought it would be something fun, something carefree, something challenging. It scares me, so therefore I think it was probably the right thing to do. Dancing is one of my passions and I've always wondered how far I could go. It's like a crash course for me. It's like living out a childhood dream.'

Nan Maureen was among the first to know that she had been accepted for the show and, as a huge fan of *Strictly Come Dancing*, Maureen was over the moon. 'I knew she'd been for the interview and then I got a call from her saying she was coming over and we were going to go out to walk the dogs,' she revealed. 'We went out and she said, "Nan, I've got something to tell you." I thought, "Oh, she's not been picked," but she said, "I'm going to do *Strictly*." I nearly did a backward somersault in the field!'

Looking forward to the show, Alesha promised she was going to thrill the audience by getting 'down and dirty' and she was itching to try out the lusty Latin dances. 'My instinct says Latin will be my favourite as I have fire in my belly and am always moving,' she admitted. 'Latin is very fast paced and fiery so I think it will suit me. Then again, when I look at the ballroom they look like princesses so I can't wait to have a go at that as well.

'I'll be getting down and dirty with the Latin and becoming a graceful princess with the ballroom.'

Her experience of dancing in pop videos, and even choreo-graphing some of Mis-Teeq's routines, made some critics feel she had an unfair advantage. But she refuted the allegation. 'They were street dances, which are completely different,' she insisted. 'That was just gyrating. So the thing I'm most worried about is not living up to my partner's expectations.' And she even admitted to a previous dance disaster in front of a mystery man. 'I was dancing in front of some man I fancied, trying to impress him, and I fell over. I'm glad to say it didn't put him off though.'

A strong believer in karma and kindness, Alesha promised a fair fight on the show, saying, 'There might be some people who are more ruthless about wanting to win but I want to win in a healthy way. It wouldn't be the end of the world if I went out in week four or five or whatever, but I am in it to win it, definitely.'

Alesha's *Strictly* journey began for real on 29 September 2007. One of fourteen celebrities to come down the hallowed staircase at BBC's Studio One, her fellow female contestants were Penny Lancaster-Stewart, Gabby Logan, Kate Garraway, Letitia Dean, Kelly Brook and Hollywood diva Stephanie Beacham. The male contestants were Kenny Logan, *Corrie* star Brian Capron, *EastEnder* Matt Di Angelo, Willie Thorne, Dominic Littlewood, John Barnes and *Blue Peter* presenter Gethin Jones.

For the first show only the male celebrities danced, although the girls managed to impress the judges with their group swing. Craig Revel Horwood called it, 'incredible dancing' and head judge Len Goodman declared, 'If that's going to be the standard it's going to be go go girls and bye bye boys.' Italian judge Bruno

Tonioli went one step further and picked Alesha and Kelly Brook out of the line up. 'The men should be afraid, very afraid, because these girls mean business,' he said. 'How to pick a jewel from all these wonderful girls? But I would say, the two hot brunettes – Alesha and Kelly. I can't wait to come back.'

Dancing the romantic rumba as the first dance, however, meant Matthew had to work on dampening some of Alesha's overabundant enthusiasm. 'Alesha's energy is never ending,' he said. 'She's bouncing off the wall and I can't control her. The rumba is slow and romantic and I need to keep her calm so she can dance the routine properly. Otherwise she'll go wild.' Alesha promised her dance partner she would focus on the night, saying, 'I'm not going to waste the moment.'

Indeed she didn't. Her dance floor debut, in a shocking pink, super-short fringed dress, brought the house down. Bruno called it, 'Sexy, raunchy, a very, very good performance'. For Craig it was, 'Absolutely gorgeous.' And Len declared, 'You're a contender.'

Despite a stunning first score of 31, Alesha was in third place after Kelly Brook and Brendan Cole, and Penny Lancaster-Stewart and Ian Waite, who both received 33. After the dance-off Stephanie Beacham left the show with a characteristically stylish farewell. 'Oh thank goodness. It's been nothing but awful,' she said. 'I have adored watching the hard work – watching it with cups in my hand – I am in such admiration for these glorious dancers. How they do it I do not know. I am so grateful to be let out of my misery.'

'I love Len,' gushed Alesha later. 'I came off the floor and I just exploded. This dancing malarkey is just great. It's brought out the competitive spirit in me.'

Nan Maureen Davies, watching from the audience, was thrilled. 'Alesha always puts her heart and soul into everything she does,' said the proud lady. 'Once she started to dance tonight, my wildest dream came true.'

For the following week, the energy levels were up as the bouncy, breezy jive was on the cards. With its high speed kicks and flicks, turns and twists, it was a dance that suited Alesha down to the ground. 'Doing the jive is like being a kid in a candy store for me,' said the excited star. 'I have so much energy I need to get out and that is the one dance that allows me to do it. I want to get out and tear up that dance floor. I want to leave everybody thinking they want to get up and jive!'

Matthew Cutler was impressed by her lack of fear for the more physical moves. 'She's not afraid to throw herself into drops and drags. She'll try anything.' But their training was interrupted when the singer sprained her knee and had to have physio to get through the week. 'It was touch and go. Thankfully I made a good recovery and things all turned out fine in the end.'

Dancing to the Blues Brothers' 'Twist It', Alesha certainly did 'shake her tail feather' in another tiny mini in luminous green. The judges were impressed. 'Another fantastic routine,' said Craig. 'The sheer energy was amazing and your finishes are perfect.'

'You're rocking, you're rolling, you're shaking your tail feather,' Arlene praised. 'I hope you get the youth of Britain up and jiving.'

'Three words,' said Len. 'Fun, fast, fantastic.' All four judges awarded a nine, giving her a score of 36 and matching the highest scores ever awarded for a second dance, for both Colin Jackson and Louisa Lytton.

'I knew when I got the 9s my family would be bouncing off the walls,' said Alesha. 'My Nan says she is going to charge the BBC for the damage to her ceiling!'

Maureen was also on hand to dole out some sage advice to her granddaughter. 'I did say to Alesha at the weekend, "That week is over. You wipe the slate clean. It's a new dance and you have to start from the beginning again," and this is exactly what she's doing. You cannot go into the next week relying on marks you got from the last week. It's a completely new dance,' she said.

Her American Smooth in week four saw Matt struggling to lose the streetwise MC in his pupil and make her more ladylike. 'We need a little less of the "yo dude!" he told her in training.

'It's like a new world to me, the Ballroom,' said Alesha. 'I was scared because I knew people might presume I would be better at the Latin and I really want to go out there and prove I can do ballroom as well.'

Although elegant and beautiful on the night, the dance got a mixed reaction, and caused a row between the judges. After Len Goodman criticized the lack of body contact and Bruno Tonioli disagreed, saying, 'For me, this was actually great. Your movement and your musicality were great. Len, I don't know what you were looking at.' Len ended up calling Bruno a 'complete doughnut' and 'prawn' and Bruno told him, rather cryptically, 'Stick one in your mouth if you want a doughnut!' Alesha hid behind her hands during what Bruce Forsyth referred to as 'Punch and Judy' and finally picked up a respectable score of 33.

'I was looking forward to doing all the dances, but the ballroom is a bit of a challenge for me because I'm not allowed to wiggle my hips,' said Alesha. 'But once you nail it, when you get to the point in training when you're really feeling the dance, you fall in love with it.'

At the bookies, Alesha had leap-frogged Kelly Brook as favourite to win and she was having the time of her life. 'People ask why me and Matt laugh so much when we're training,' she told *The Sun*. 'I just think, what's the point of doing it if you're not going to have fun? . . . I feel really good, I'm loving doing *Strictly* and it's a big turnaround for me.'

Despite her consistently high scores, however, she wasn't complacent about her chances of reaching the final. 'There's such a high standard this year. It's dangerous to underestimate anyone this early because they can progress so quickly. You can say Penny stands out because she's got grace and height, or Gabby because she's got suppleness or Kelly because she's sexy – everybody's got something that makes them stand out.'

Her own particular quality, she reckoned, was 'feistiness, probably! Or passion. I do put my all into it'. Her energy level, she admitted, made the hours in hair and make-up, getting 'more bling than P. Diddy' a chore but, more used to denim minis and biker boots, she was revelling in the sparkly dresses and high heels.

'The dresses are gorgeous, but then they get out the cuffs and the necklace and the earrings and I'm thinking, "OK, less is more!" But it does look good on camera and I am enjoying the opportunity to get dressed up.'

'Alesha is an absolute dream,' said *Strictly Come Dancing* stylist Su Judd, 'because she came in with so many great ideas, and loved the whole process. Both she and Kelly absolutely loved it.'

In week five, Alesha had to locate her inner lady once again for the Foxtrot, and this time she had a couple of critical spectators at the training sessions. Grandmothers Clem and Maureen got together to lay on a 1940s-style tea party with cakes and sandwiches, while Matt looking dashing in a wartime military uniform. But the two ladies weren't impressed by the constant giggling going on between the dancing duo, scolding Alesha for not taking it seriously enough. She admitted she was struggling at first.

'On Monday and Tuesday I was a nightmare,' she revealed in a *GMTV* interview that week. 'I moaned all day, I just couldn't get it. I wasn't tired – I love the whole physical side of it – but I struggled to understand the dance.'

The couple was already training for six hours a day and Alesha said she was trying to persuade Matthew to train on Sundays as well, 'but he's not having it!'

'You never feel you've done enough. You always feel you could do better if you had more time,' she went on.

And she also revealed that her time performing with Mis-Teeq had done nothing to calm her nerves on the show. 'With the girls I was in my comfort zone, but with this I feel like a small fish in a big pond and I'm out of my depth, so before the show my hands start sweating and I genuinely get really nervous. I think everybody does but there's a real buzz backstage.'

Despite having the highest score of the series, Matthew said that he was eager to beat his best. 'I definitely want to beat that score and be at the top every week. That's my goal.'

'He worries about that more than I do,' replied Alesha.

Yet again, when Saturday night came, Alesha pulled it out of the bag and delivered a fabulous Foxtrot which had 'heavenly elegance' according to Bruno. Craig called it 'sensitive, honest, loving, beautiful' and 'absolutely gorgeous'. Even Arlene was overwhelmed, 'You are the real deal,' she told the emotional star, who was in tears. 'You glimmer, you shimmer, you shine and you bring warmth to everything you do.' At the top of the leader board once more with 36 points, Alesha was a sure thing for the final. 'I was so emotional,' she explained later, 'because I thought I was going to get slated.'

She wasn't the only one in tears. Nan Clem, who was in the audience, admitted, 'I was so proud of her that a little bit of tears came from my eyes. It was beautiful.'

After the show Bruno enthused, 'Alesha was like an angel tonight,' and Lilia Kopylova, speaking on *Strictly*'s companion show, *It Takes Two*, had her money on the former rapper. 'Alesha is my big hope,' said the series-three champ, 'everything she does is amazing.'

As she blossomed on the dance floor, Alesha's confidence, inevitably damaged by Harvey's affair with Javine, began to return. 'I have days when I'm not as confident, but to be a success is to be a good person,' she said in the *Daily Mirror*. And the constant praise from the judges was helping too.

'Judge Craig Revel Horwood said I was sexy without flaunting it,' said the delighted dancer. 'I love that. You don't have to get all your bits out. You can be sexy by how you carry yourself. I'm not there to compare myself to anyone. I don't see the girls as a threat. They're good company. I don't need to get my skin out to compete. If I see a beautiful girl, I don't feel threatened by her. It's not in my character.'

In fact Alesha was making plenty of new friends amongst the dancers and celebrities, and her infectious, guttural laugh could be heard ringing around the corridors of the BBC every Saturday night, especially if Letitia Dean was around.

'Letitia is hilarious,' said Alesha. 'I tell them to keep her away from me on show day if I have a serious dance. She cracks me up! Penny is very motherly and has a lovely aura. I think when Penny dances, she really feels the dance. She has a beautiful spirit.

'I haven't spent much time with Kelly [Brook] but she's a sweet girl. She does get a hard time but she's absolutely harmless. She likes dancing and doesn't have to say sorry for what she looks like. And she's always happy, which is really nice.'

Unlike many of her fellow contestants, Alesha said she was still waiting for the toned tummy and weight loss to kick in. But being a perfect size 10, she was happy with way she looked. 'My tummy isn't flat – I'd rather eat than starve to look good in a crop top.'

A superb salsa in week six saw the real Alesha take to the floor. The party dance allowed her to wiggle her hips and really let herself go and she looked amazing in a fuschia pink feathered dress. With both her grandmothers in the audience she brought the whole studio to the party with a dance that had Bruno taking off his jacket and declaring it, 'Hot! Hot! Hot!'

'Everyone should do salsa as exercise,' she said after the dance. 'Forget going down the gym and running on the machine, go to the salsa club.'

Despite an impressive score of 35, however, Alesha and Matthew were knocked down to the middle of the leader board by three couples who tied at the top with 36. Matt Di Angelo and Flavia Cacace, Kelly Brook and Brendan Cole and Gethin Jones and Camilla Dallerup were proving stiff competition.

Never one to rest on her laurels, Alesha fought back with style. A stunning waltz in week seven put her firmly back on top with a score of 38, including her first two tens from Arlene and

Bruno. 'I was swept away on the sea of love, beauty, elegance, the perfect combination. I'm in love,' said Bruno, and Craig admitted it actually gave him goosebumps.

'Has that ever happened before to you?' asked Bruce.

'No, not on this show!' joked Craig.

Alesha was ecstatic, saying, 'And it's ballroom! I can't believe it.'

The following week the couple watched backstage as close rivals Matt and Flavia performed a sizzling salsa that had the judges cooing and landed them their first tens. With a score of 38, they nestled in at the top spot, confident that this was their week. But Alesha wasn't having that. Her cha-cha cha to Beyoncé's 'Crazy in Love' wowed the audience with an amazing showbiz opening, shimmies and fast, precise steps. Len called it her 'best dance yet', Craig told her, 'You are Fab-U-lous!' and a very excited Bruno leapt out of his seat to declare, 'My pulse is racing, my heart is pounding. It's diva time!'

'From what I am seeing tonight, this is a two-horse competition,' Arlene predicted. 'And you are one of the horses.'

The other frontrunner, Matt Di Angelo, was not so thrilled when Alesha pipped him to the post with her amazing score of 39. 'I was the King of Dance,' he complained, 'then Alesha has blown us out of the water!'

'I love that routine,' Alesha said later. 'Matthew and I both adore the song – but I have to thank Matt and Flavia for giving us the extra boost to perform it. Their salsa before our dance the first time was so strong that it really lifted the crowd. That gave us a lift too so we really went for it.

'We got a higher score and Matt said, "Thanks 'Lish, you couldn't let me have my moment in the sun!"'

With tens from all but Craig, Alesha was on a roll. 'I remember being at home and watching someone getting a ten was special, so to be here and actually getting them myself is wicked. '*Strictly* has taken over my life, I wake up in the morning and I don't even have any food in my house because I haven't had time to go shopping.'

As well as raising her profile in the papers, Alesha's dancing feet earned her a few famous fans. 'There's so much energy in Alesha. I think she's wicked,' said former contestant Zoë Ball, and Lisa Snowdon, who would take part in the following series, said, 'I absolutely adore her. I just can't take my eyes off her.'

Due to the death of her father, Kelly Brook, another contender for the title, withdrew from the show after the eighth week, leaving the way clear for Matt Di Angelo and Alesha to storm to the finals, with Gethin Jones breathing down their necks. Instead of rubbing her hands together at the thought that she'd seen off another of her rivals, the kind-hearted singer was deeply upset that they had gone.

'It was really horrible when Kelly and Brendan left,' she said. 'It felt really weird not having them in the show. Brendan was like a force of nature with the judges. So losing him was like having a pantomime with the villain missing. The atmosphere really changed that week and Kelly was really missed. And it was sad for her because she's got a passion for dance and it all ended in such an unfortunate way.'

Alesha's euphoria at the score soon disappeared as training began for the tango. The pressure of the competition finally got to her and her usual happy-go-lucky demeanour disappeared as she went into meltdown. Tearful and blue, she said the tens had merely added to the nerves: 'The pressure is on. They make me nervous.' But the panel was once more enraptured by her terrific tango.

'The tantalizing tango temptress triumphs!' commented Arlene. Although Len was critical of her footwork, he admitted it was because he expected nothing less than perfection, but Bruno declared, 'For me you are a divine dance idol and I can't take my eyes off you.' And Craig marvelled at her ability to switch between the two dance disciplines. 'Confident, controlled, an entire brilliant package I think you are. You have managed to master both ballroom and Latin. You're just fantastic.'

'I was so scared,' Alesha admitted. 'It was the hardest dance I've ever done.' She scooped a score of 38 but, ever the perfectionist, told presenter Tess Daly. 'I loved it. I just wish I could do it better.'

'Alesha is really determined to always go out there and do the best she can,' commented Matthew Cutler.

Despite Craig's comments on her ability to be an all-rounder, Alesha admitted she was shocked that her ballroom scores were higher than her Latin. 'It freaks me out, but the weeks I've got the highest scores are also the weeks we've really struggled.'

With only five celebrities left, each couple had to perform two dances for the first time in the series. Alesha followed her tango with a salsa, which left Arlene unimpressed, calling her 'lazy-legged', but left Craig in awe. 'I could watch you all night, I really could. Absolutely sensational,' he said, and Bruno raved, 'You're like a young Josephine Baker. Fantastic exoticism.'

With a score of 36, bringing the total to 74, the couple tied at the top with Gethin and Camilla. They waited in the spotlight to hear their names and Alesha was soon jumping for joy.

They had made the quarter-finals.

CHAPTER TEN

Having a Ball

While Alesha was tearing up the dance floor and gaining a bigger fan base each week, she and Harvey were back in contact, if only to talk about the divorce.

'He wished me good luck,' she told *The Sun*. 'He always told me I'd be brilliant on *Strictly*. I even had my mother-in-law and his aunties come down to the show because I'm still really close to his family. I have forgiven Harvey. We're adults and we're dealing with it as maturely as two people can.'

In an interview with the *Daily Mirror*, Harvey's new love, seven months pregnant with his child, also wished her well. 'Alesha is doing brilliantly and good on her,' said Javine. 'It might sound strange for me to say this but I genuinely want her to be happy and I really hope she wins.'

Despite unfounded rumours in the papers that Alesha was dating fellow contestant Matt Di Angelo, she had remained single since the split and, a year on, was coming to terms with the idea of dating again. The Matt rumours she said were, 'just comical. I feel like I'm old enough to be Matt's mother. To be honest I'd been hoping there would be someone I fancied on the crew. But there wasn't. Never mind.'

'Dancing makes you feel really sexy,' she told the *People*. 'I call it foreplay without the finale. When you're dancing with somebody all day and spending that much time up close together, it makes you feel very sexual. You're more flirty than you would normally be and I've definitely become a very flirty person since I started doing the show.'

But, with her newfound love of Latin and ballroom, she stipulated that any suitor would have to display some skill on the dance floor to catch her eye. 'I'll be hitting the salsa clubs now so the men will have to show some pretty good moves to win me over.'

As the public got behind her on the show, Alesha's broken heart was mending fast and she was, once again, the gorgeous, gregarious girl that had so charmed everybody she met in the Mis-Teeq days. In fact, she was over Harvey, so much so that she was beginning to appreciate many aspects of the single life.

'I'm not ready for a relationship yet,' she confessed in the *People*. 'I'm just enjoying single life and it really does have its benefits. You're your own person, you can do what you like, you can flirt with whoever you like. I do want to settle down in the future, though. The next person I get in a relationship with, it can't be casual, it's got to be the real thing, so I'd rather just wait and take my time.'

She did admit to having her broody moments though. 'Emma Bunton brought her baby, Beau, in to meet me on Saturday night. And, oh my God, he's gorgeous. But I feel I want to do so much before I have children.'

In another interview she was looking forward to the opportunities that would inevitably arise through her *Strictly* exposure, and was pleased she could decide which ones to take without consulting a partner. I've been on dates but I'm happy being single. It's fun being able to flirt with people,' she revealed. 'I feel quite emotionally sane, which is good, because as any woman knows, being in a relationship is an emotional roller coaster.

'When I was in the band and we travelled a lot, it was tough being away from your partner. But I don't have that worry any more. If I had a call tomorrow asking me to go to the States, I could do it. I've got this opportunity in my life to do what I want to do and I feel I have to take it.'

At that moment, what she really wanted to do was carry on dancing. In the quarter-finals, having already scored more tens than any previous celebrity, smashing Mark Ramprakash's record from the previous series, Alesha was chomping at the bit and raring to go.

'I know this sounds cheesy, but I really do feel like I've already won just by being on the show!' she said in an interview with *The Guardian*. 'Everyone's got a chance, because personality counts for such a lot. But the competition isn't with other people, it's within yourself, you're always trying to do better than you did before. Take Letitia, for example, she's been vulnerable on the show, and she's been on her own personal journey and she's wonderful.'

But with only four couples left and two dances to learn each week, the pressure was on. Alesha and Matt were now training or dancing seven days a week, and even the ultra-energetic Alesha was beginning to feel the strain. 'There is stress,' she told *The Guardian*. 'You get upset for no reason, just due to the exhaustion. I felt teary all day yesterday . . . It's just so overwhelming sometimes.'

But she vowed that she would put all her remaining energy into the dances. 'At this stage of the competition we are working day and night. The competition is fierce but I have got fuel left in the tank. I don't want the fairytale to end.'

While she adored dance partner Matthew Cutler, she confessed, the couple's proximity for such intense periods of time did mean they were getting on each other's nerves occasionally. 'I have now spent 320 hours in Matt's company,' she revealed. 'I work with him from 10am until 10pm. It's all so last minute. Even now, I don't know all the steps for one of the dances I'm doing on this week's show. Matthew can be quite strict with me. He actually sent me home yesterday. I wasn't happy about it. He annoys me sometimes, but it's through absolutely no fault of his. He's male and I'm female. Sometimes we flirt – a bit. We get on extremely well.'

Although there was no hint of romance between the two, she told one magazine that Matthew, who is separated from wife and dance partner Nicole, was the most fanciable guy on the set.

'I wake up every morning and look forward to training with him,' she said. 'I love him. I have a passion for dance, for raising money and for having fun, and it's been great to do that with him. When I have to stop dancing with him I'll be very sad.'

And she clearly loved their friendly flirting. 'The ballroom dancing is very sexy,' she told *FHM*. 'You can lean in and whisper to each other while you're on the floor. The Latin dancing is very physical and flirty. Just go to a salsa club!'

She also told them she felt sorry for men watching the show because they couldn't always admit it to their mates. 'I've had sneaky messages from guys on Facebook saying how much they enjoy the show, but have to go to the pub afterwards for a pint to restore their masculinity,' she laughed. 'I feel sorry for men sometimes. It's so odd that you're not really allowed to do things like watch dancing or cry.'

Gethin and Camilla kicked off the quarter-finals with an elegant American Smooth which landed them 38 points. Alesha and Matthew were next on the floor with a dreamy Viennese waltz to the *Cats* classic 'Memory', which had an overwhelmed Bruno gasping, 'The fairytale is just beginning. How can anyone resist such beauty and such radiance? In your face you were telling the story of the song. I lived the song with you.' To which Arlene added, 'You turn a simple Viennese waltz into a magical memory.'

'If you don't get four tens for that I'm going to go home and pickle me walnuts!' pledged Len. Indeed, his walnuts were duly pickled after Craig and Arlene stuck to a score of nine each, giving her 38.

The dress Alesha wore for the dance would later be named as her favourite from the show. 'All my costumes have been amazing but my Viennese waltz dress was one of my absolute faves. It was pink with lots of layers and it made me feel like Cinderella. It was beautiful.'

Later Alesha found out Elaine Paige, who had sung the original song, was in the audience. 'I'm so glad I didn't know she was here,' Alesha said. 'That would have made me even more nervous.' But Elaine was delighted. 'I was stunned to hear that song,' she said. 'And she danced beautifully to that beautiful melody.'

Closest rival Matt suffered a terrible attack of nerves and messed up both his routines, ending up at the bottom of the leader board, but dark horse Gethin had had a breakthrough, gaining 37 for his lively jive, giving him a total of 75 points. Before Alesha and Matthew took to the floor for their Paso Doble, the judges were heaping praise on the hot favourite.

'She does class and she does sexy. She does beauty and she does beast. What more do you want?' said Bruno. 'Alesha is the one who has been consistent, and consistently consistent . . . Yes, she has problems, we all do. But she is full of sass and she's hot, hot, hot.'

'Alesha's waltz is poetry,' said Arlene.

But Len warned, 'Alesha is the one everyone wants to beat. Everyone wants to knock her off the pedestal. In every series of *Strictly Come Dancing* every celebrity, no matter how good, has had one dance that is their nemesis. It could well be the Paso Doble?'

Apparently not. Dressed in a stunning green and gold flamenco dress, Alesha stamped her way through the dance of the matador beautifully and impressed the judges. 'Attack, passion, drama, I loved it,' said Craig.

'Dramatic. You felt it and we could see that in your eyes,' said Arlene.

No one was more surprised by the positive comments than Alesha, who confessed backstage, 'We really messed up. Badly.' And after Tess Daly commented that was the first time the couple had gone wrong during a routine, Alesha replied, 'No it isn't!'

'I was so scared, I just didn't want to show it,' admitted Alesha later. 'The last twenty seconds of that routine was made up.'

Asked how much she wanted to win the competition, the singer joked, 'More than food!' and Matthew added, 'And that's a lot.' A score of 36 put them second on the leader board, but after Matt di Angelo was voted through by a sympathetic public, Alesha got her first taste of the dreaded dance-off against Letitia

Dean and Darren Bennett. 'We all knew there was a fifty-fifty chance. I never felt we were safe.'

Len was astonished. 'I can't believe they're in the bottom two,' he marvelled. Her second Viennese waltz of the evening was declared 'near perfect' by Craig, and Arlene remarked, 'I never want to stop watching her dance.' The judges were unanimous and Alesha was saved.

Later she revealed the full extent of their mistake in the Paso. 'I made up the last thirty seconds, but because Matthew is so brilliant, he just followed me and we got through it. People said afterwards we did a good job of covering it up. We had a good giggle about that when we finished filming.'

As she prepared for the semi-finals in mid December, the UK's new dancing queen was having the time of her life. Offers of work were already pouring in, including secret talks for a starring role in the West End production *Chicago*. The pain and heartache of the previous Christmas had vanished amidst a flurry of sequins, diamanté and glitter, and Alesha could hardly believe that just one year before she had been an emotional wreck. 'I've had ups and downs this year,' she said. 'I went through a divorce, but since September it's been one of my best years. I've fallen in love with ballroom dancing through *Strictly Come Dancing*. I don't want the show to end. People keep asking me whether I want to be in the final, and obviously I do, but that also means the end of the show. I'll miss dancing with Matt, especially.'

And with her profile now at its highest peak, Alesha was looking to the future and hoping to use the opportunity to inspire others. 'I'd love to have my own TV show one day, something more serious that deals with current affairs, something inspirational for the younger generation,' she said. 'But I'm still a music girl: I've got music in my heart.'

Although still single, Alesha was also making plans for a family in the next six years, but first she was keen to seize the day. 'I do want a family one day. My dream is to settle down and have a family by the time I'm about thirty-five, so this is my opportunity to see the world again and have fun . . . I feel really good, I'm loving doing *Strictly* and it's a big turnaround for me.'

As she got closer to the prize, her ever-present grandmothers were getting more and more excited and couldn't be more proud. After Alesha said she was dancing for her nans, Maureen commented, 'It just pulls at my heartstrings, but once she gets on the floor and start dances, my heart just fills with joy. It's wonderful watching her . . . Alesha is a girl who will put her heart and soul into everything she does, and I knew she would do the best that she possibly could with the dancing, but it's wonderful to see that she's doing so well.'

Behind the scenes, all that Latin passion was getting to Maureen too. 'It's even had an effect on my family,' Alesha revealed. 'I rang my Nan for some advice on my cha-cha and she said, "Just give it some sex." I couldn't believe I was hearing this from my grandma!'

With her pal Letitia gone, Alesha was going into the semi-finals as the only female celebrity left, which only fuelled her fighting spirit. 'For the last two years of *SCD* a guy has won, so I'd love to give the boys a run for their money. Isn't it about time the girls got back on top?' she asked.

And she was aware that TV heartthrobs Gethin and Matt were serious competition and that their legion of young female fans could cost her the title. 'Oh, the boys. The boys!' she told *The Guardian*. 'The girls out there will fancy the boys, and vote for them. If I don't win, that's fine; that'll mean it wasn't meant to be.

In an interview with the *Sunday Mirror* Alesha admitted, 'Matt is good looking but he reminds me of my little brother, so I couldn't believe it when a rumour started that we were dating. But underneath that boy-next-door image, he and Flavia are strong contenders. I love watching Gethin and Camilla dance. Gethin has got a big following – women always vote for men rather than other women. But there's nothing wrong with a bit of healthy competition.'

While the nation tingled to her tango and cheered her cha-cha-cha, the pop star was not convinced she had what it takes to lift the trophy. 'You're your own worst critic. I watch myself afterwards and I absolutely cringe. The only one I can watch without cringing is the waltz. I am a perfectionist who has never reached perfection.'

For the semi-finals Alesha and Matthew had to tackle the Argentine tango and the quickstep. The dances were beginning to bring out the actress in Alesha and she was enjoying the role-playing aspect immensely. 'For the tango I can be a sexy, seducing senorita and then I can go and do the quickstep and be the smiley, bubbly person I am,' she said before the show.

In fact, the quickstep was the first dance of the evening, and the stunning singer looked the epitome of class as she glided round the floor in a sparkling white floor-length gown with long matching gloves.

'You might be the last girl standing but you look like the First Lady of dance,' gasped an enraptured Bruno.

'Fantastic,' smiled Craig. 'Full of syncopated steps, difficult steps, and what's more, you made it look really easy. That stuff is so hard. No buts.'

'You are about to turn this semi-final into a killer competition,' Arlene told the grinning girl. 'That neat and nippy footwork turned the nip in the air outside hot.'

A score of 38 started the semis with a bang, but Alesha admitted the run-up to evening, in the wake of the dance-off, had been tough. And she was suffering from a strong attack of nerves. 'It's so exciting, and you want to enjoy every moment, but actually I feel a bit sick,' she told presenter Tess Daly.

With Matt and Flavia tangoing their way to 35 and Gethin and Camilla's Paso Doble gaining 34, Alesha and Matthew started the second half on top. Their dramatic Argentine tango, to the appropriate strains of 'I'd Be Surprisingly Good For You' from *Evita*, was another triumph and the sultry singer pouted her way through the routine in an eye-catching scarlet tango dress, once more reducing nan Maureen to tears in the audience. But the Argentine sparked a bit of argy-bargy among the judges.

'The storytelling was amazing,' said Craig. 'You made that into a three-act play. But I did feel a little let down, only because it lacked a certain amount of attack.'

'That was subtlety!' argued Bruno.

Arlene was on Craig's side, however. 'Without doubt you are one of the best storytellers we have ever had on *Strictly*. This dance is about seduction and longing, and the nation was feeling that. But the knees were bent on the scissor lift and the caressing of the floor was not as perfect as I would like it to be and – Len and Bruno before you say anything – that's MY opinion.'

'We do respect your opinion,' fired back Len. 'Even if, sometimes, it's wrong. For me the Argentine tango is about the flirtiness of it, sidling up behind him, tapping him on the shoulder, come on big boy! I thought that was a delight.'

'You're so common!' said a miffed Arlene as Alesha fell about laughing.

'For me that was so focussed,' added Bruno. 'The irresistible power of subtle seduction. You never lost your performance all the way through. It was great.'

Another 38 left the couple with a magnificent score of 76.

After Matt's mistakes in the quarter-finals, the *EastEnder* came back stronger than ever, snatching the first perfect forty of the competition with his waltz, but even that wasn't enough to knock Alesha off the top spot. Gethin and Camilla waltzed into the sunset after a dance-off against Matt and Flavia and the final battle was about to begin.

CHAPTER ELEVEN

A Phoenix Rises

Alesha's fairytale was coming true. The first name put through to the final, the tomboy MC had been transformed into a true queen of the ballroom, brimming with elegance and grace. 'The feeling of getting through to the final is just incredible,' she grinned on *Strictly Come Dancing*'s *It Takes Two*. 'When Bruce said my name I just started crying. I will treasure that moment forever. I want to go out with a bang.'

Whatever happens, she insisted, she had been saved by the show. 'I actually thought 2007 was going to be crap,' she said. 'But because of *Strictly* my confidence is back – dancing actually saved me. I've got the real me back. I'm ending this year on a high.'

Characteristically selfless, she admitted she was desperate to get her hands on the mirror ball trophy, if only for the sake of professional partner Matthew. 'The best Christmas present I could get him would be to win the show,' she told the *Sunday Mirror*. 'But second to that I have already given him a framed engraved picture of us dancing together.'

The judges clearly thought Alesha had more than an even chance at the title. 'Pound for pound Alesha is one of the best dancers *Strictly* has ever seen,' said choreographer Arlene Phillips.

'Matthew Cutler is the king of Latin American,' said Bruno. 'He's got more awards than Helen Mirren!'

The training levels had now reached their peak, with ten hours a day spent at the north London studio, which had become her second home. The singer, who would later admit that she had lost a stone, said she was feeling fitter than ever.

'I don't know how much weight I've lost because I don't do scales,' she said before the final. 'I don't do diets and I don't calorie-count. But I do feel like I've lost a layer of something. My muscles are stronger, I'm more toned and I feel fit.'

Alesha's success meant she had become the role model for black and mixed-race youngsters, a goal she had long striven for, but she had come to represent much more. She was an example to women who had overcome adversity and to kids who were struggling to make it out of a humble background.

'I represent the girl whose mum couldn't afford to send her to stage school, but who's getting the chance to catch up when she's twenty-nine,' she said in the *Sunday Mirror*. 'I come from a single-parent family and nothing was ever given to me – I've had to work for everything I've achieved. It sounds corny, but the only reason I did *Strictly* was to learn to dance. So whatever happens, I feel like a winner. And I'm happier than ever.'

While her dancing on the programme was winning her the votes, she conceded that much of the warmth and female following she had been receiving was down to the circumstances in which she found herself before the show.

'I think people like to see women rise from situations like that,' she said. 'My feeling is, if you're a good person and you've got your morals and someone does something like that to you, then you've got nothing to hang your head in shame about. I think a lot of women have been very supportive because they understand what I've been through.'

While her devastating marriage break-up and public rebirth may have won her plenty of support, Alesha didn't feel this was the reason she had got so far in the competition. 'I could sense the support and it felt good,' she admitted a year later. 'But my spirit was upbeat so I don't think I ever asked for the sympathy vote.'

Going into the final of the most glamorous competition on earth, it wasn't sympathy she needed, just nerves of steel – and perhaps a little Dutch courage.

In an interview with the *Daily Mirror* before the show, she revealed a rather naughty backstage secret: 'I probably shouldn't be telling you this, but it's the last night so it doesn't matter any more,' she giggled. 'We drink white wine backstage before the show and tell the bosses it's apple juice!'

For the final, she had to perfect five dances, including two the couple had done before, a Viennese waltz which she and Matthew would perform alongside Matt and Flavia, a freestyle dance to a track of the judges' choosing, and a show dance. The couple chose the stately waltz, which had earned them 38, the cha-cha-cha which had been awarded 39 and a lively, sassy jive for the judges' track.

'I love the song "A Time For Us" by Johnny Mathis,' said Alesha of the waltz that had famously given Craig goosebumps. 'The dress was beautiful and we managed to get all the steps right. I also managed to get into the emotion so I felt really great about the performance.'

'I am happy she's chosen the waltz because it really *did* give me goosebumps,' commented Craig Revel Horwood on *It Takes Two*. 'The only thing she needs to do to get all the tens is to make sure the footwork is perfect. We tend to look at her top line, because

Bouncing back: Alesha lends her support to Nickelodeon's 'See Something, Say Something' anti-bullying campaign.

Naturally sporty, Alesha was in her element at the Celebrity Soccer Six Tournament at Upton Park in 2003.

Championing Help a London Child, Alesha and Johnny Vaughan launch the BUPA Great Capital Run in 2008.

Alesha and her dance partner Matthew Cutler, with whom she won the fifth series of *Strictly Come Dancing* in December 2007.

The cast of *Strictly* receive the award for Most Popular Talent Show at the 2008 National Television Awards.

A star is reborn: Alesha at the BAFTA Awards with Bruce Forsyth and his wife Wilnelia.

Alesha wins the Ultimate Confidence Award at the Cosmopolitan Ultimate Women of the Year Awards 2008, supported by *Strictly*'s Craig Revel-Horwood and Matthew Cutler.

Flying solo: Asylum Records and her manager Malcolm Blair (pictured) helped establish Alesha as an artist in her own right.

The Alesha Show: performing to fans at G-A-Y in 2008.

Dubbed the 'British Beyoncé' by Bruce Forsyth, Alesha wows fans at Radio 1's Big Weekend in 2009.

In fine company: Alesha (second from right) with a host of other celebrities including Michael Sheen (far right), Rob Brydon (third from right) and Jamelia (fourth from left) at the Prince's Trust Celebrate Success Awards in 2009.

A good sport: Alesha with MCC members at Lord's Cricket Ground in 2009.

With Marvin from JLS at T4 on the Beach in Weston-super-Mare.

Still smiling: Alesha ascends Mount Kilimanjaro for Comic Relief in 2009.

With her fellow celebrities Alesha raised over £1 million to help the fight against malaria in Tanzania.

The Kilimanjaro team were invited to Downing Street to meet Gordon Brown.

Alesha and former *Strictly* judge
Arlene Phillips pictured together
in 2008. A year later, Alesha took
Arlene's position on the panel.

The new series begins: Brucie
leaves the press conference at
which Alesha is officially declared
the new judge.

Another series, another set of contestants: (from l-r) Laila Rouass,
Phil Tufnell, Zoe Lucker, Joe Calzaghe, Craig Kelly, Natalie Cassidy
and Lynda Bellingham.

Strictly stunning: the smile that has endeared Alesha to the nation.

she's radiant, but we also have to look at it from a technical point of view. I want her to be perfect. The cha-cha-cha is one of her favourite genres because she's brilliant at it. She has such energy and style and she just wants to go for it. I know now she's a bit more relaxed about it and she'll just go mental over this.'

For the judges' choice dance, both couples must perform to the same song. For the Alesha vs. Matt contest they chose the upbeat T-Rex number 'I Love to Boogie'. And for Alesha's show dance the couple chose Bonnie Tyler's 'Holding Out For A Hero', a belting rock ballad with an upbeat tempo.

'That's a mad song,' laughed Craig. 'Bonnie Tyler goes mad in that and I'm sure Matt is going to have a lot of fun throwing Alesha around to that.'

Back in the training room, in the week before the final, Alesha was having anything but fun. Exhausted from intensive training, and barely sleeping because of crippling nerves, her body was beginning to rebel. 'I have bruises on my hands, arms and legs,' she admitted to *The Sun*. 'I'm getting through on willpower and adrenalin. We have been working harder than anyone, from 10am until 10pm – day in day out.

'On Thursday I thought I had done my back in. It went into spasm and I really thought God was against me. I went to physio and felt in such pain I thought I'd be out of the final.

'I had to learn the show dance sitting down. I was lying on the floor, crying in pain and I started to have a panic attack – but I got through it. A song that Matt and Flavia are dancing to came on and I jumped straight back up.'

The day before the final she was sick on the studio floor, and for a moment she believed she wouldn't make it to the studio, and she admitted that the strain of the latter weeks of the competition was getting to her.

'It's been a tough few weeks in the last stages of the competition. There have literally been blood, sweat and tears — actually, quite a lot of tears. It's been part and parcel of being a woman. I didn't even know why I was crying half the time.'

Two years on, however, she admitted on a chat show that the reason for her sickness was slightly less innocent than straightforward nerves. 'On the Thursday night Matt Cutler and I went out for dinner because we were celebrating coming to the end of the show,' Alesha told Justin Lee Collins in 2009. 'There was a party going on in the hotel. Somebody came down the stairs, spotted us and invited us up to the party. We went and got really drunk and on the Friday before the final, I threw up on the *SCD* dance floor! I've never told anyone that. I couldn't tell the producers I was drunk. I told them it was nerves. But really it was alcohol! It happened two or three times. I felt so ashamed, because the carpet was so nice. And everyone knows I like a clean house!'

On the night of 22 December 2007, as the nation held its collective breath, the dancing queen pulled herself together, following Matt and Flavia's American Smooth with a beautiful waltz. 'The waltz was the pinnacle for me so we've chosen to do that again in the final,' she said on the show. 'It was a very special moment so I really want to get out there and capture that moment again.'

That's precisely what she did. In a shimmering white and silver dress, she enchanted the audience and the judges.

'It sent shivers down my spine,' said Bruno. 'This is truly becoming an enchanted evening.'

'It must be catching,' agreed Craig. 'Goosebumps again! You've really tidied up your footwork. I found it flawless.'

'Triple A,' said Arlene. 'Alesha Absolutely Amazing! What I want everybody at home to remember is that Alesha came into the show with absolutely no dance training and she is just heavenly.'

For once, however, Len Goodman played the bad guy, picking up on a couple of footwork faults and saying, to loud boos from the audience, 'It wasn't flawless.'

With more tens than anyone else before – with a total of fourteen already – the couple were yet to receive one from acerbic Aussie Craig. That was about to change. With a ten from him, Bruno and Arlene, Alesha racked up a score of 39.

Matt and Flavia quickly fought back by matching that score with a sizzling salsa which Bruno remarked, 'chased those winter blues away'. Then Alesha and Matthew took to the floor once more with a repeat of their highest scoring dance. 'The cha-cha was such an exciting dance for us. We got three tens and we'd love to get that fourth from Craig.'

'If this cha-cha-cha was in the West End it would run forever because I want to watch it over and over and over again,' said Bruno.

'That cha-cha was cheekier than *Chicago* and flashier than *Flashdance*,' gushed an excited Arlene.

'In the past people have asked me who is the best girl celebrity we've had and I always say Jill Halfpenny,' head judge Len told the astonished dancer. 'Henceforth, Alesha Dixon.'

'You were wild!' laughed Matthew Cutler as they left the stage, and the wild child earned 38 points, one fewer than the first cha-cha.

For the judges' choice, a head-to-head contest, Matt and Flavia chose a quickstep and Alesha and Matthew the jive. 'We chose the jive because Alesha has bundles of energy and I'm hoping she will go out there and explode,' explained Matthew, and Alesha promised, 'I'm gonna go out there and get the party started! Matt and Flavia had better watch out 'cos Dixon and Cutler is comin' at ya!

But Craig warned, 'It's a side-by-side comparison and there's nowhere to hide.'

Both couples delivered stunning routines and the judges agreed it was the most unpredictable final that they had ever seen. 'Matt you are up against one of the best female celebrities we've ever had on this show and yet you are managing to hold your own,' commented Len. 'Alesha, you are born to perform and every dance is an absolute knockout. You both came out and dominated the floor.'

'This is one of the tightest positions we've been in because you guys are so close and Matt you have improved so much,' added Craig, and Arlene chirped, 'Both couples here are in it to win it and it's really exciting.'

Matching scores of 35 put Alesha at the top of the leader board, with the Viennese waltz and show dances to come.

'We are two points behind but with two dances left, it's totally within our grasp,' said Matt Di Angelo.

'The two dances left are actually the most difficult to do,' said Alesha. 'The show dance is risky. I just feel I need to get out there, do the job and start praying!'

With the judges' scores in, at 112 and 119 respectively, the rest was up to the public as the last two dances are not given points. The two couples shared the floor for the Viennese waltz, which had Bruno once more brimming with admiration. 'This has got to be the closest fought final ever,' he enthused. 'You two are the best of British and what young people should be all about. I am lost for words, for once.'

Craig picked up the theme, 'I've never known such electricity in the room and that's due to the way you guys dance. I believe you are both running on a parallel at the moment and that's extraordinary because we've never had that.'

'Matt, you've proved to everyone you deserve to be in the final tonight,' said Len. 'Alesha, you've been Miss Consistency throughout. It doesn't matter what dance is thrown at you, you come out with elegance and poise. You're the complete package.'

Three of her biggest fans, her mum and two grandmothers, were, of course, in the audience to watch her and Clem told her, 'I am very proud of you, Alesha. If you win this competition tonight, I will be the happiest nanny in the world.'

'It's been a sheer delight watching you dance,' added Maureen. 'Good luck, sweetheart. I love you very much and I hope you win.'

Matt was first with a rocking cha-cha show dance to the Lenny Kravitz track, 'Are You Gonna Go My Way?' and it looked like things might go his way when Len raved, 'You nailed it!' Arlene called it 'dynamite' and Bruno told him, 'You rocked!'

Then Alesha was unleashed. Starting the dance in a deep purple dress with arms crossed and legs covered, she raised her arms so that the 'skirt' became a dramatic backdrop exposing her impossibly long, shapely legs. The audience went wild. The ninety-second routine included numerous lifts, fast footwork and stunning lines and ended with Matthew lifting

Alesha above him by one leg and then letting her fall into his arms.

'I need a hero,' remarked Arlene, as she uncharacteristically leapt out of her chair. 'Tonight, Alesha, you are my heroine.'

'This was more than a dance,' shouted Bruno. 'It was a stunning, epic performance!'

Alesha clapped in agreement as Len commented, 'There can only be one winner, but for me, tonight there is no loser, because Matt and yourself put on such a great show.'

The public vote counted, the two couples stood in the spotlight for an agonizing twelve seconds until they heard, 'It's Alesha and Matthew.' An ecstatic Alesha leapt into Matthew's arms kicking her legs in sheer excitement as Matt Di Angelo comforted Flavia and the judges gave the couple a standing ovation. In the audience Alesha's family jumped for joy and hugged each other as the series' other stars mobbed the stage. 'I'm so happy. I'm lost for words,' said Alesha's tearful mum Beverley. 'This means the world to her and she's worked so hard.'

Even as Bruce Forsyth pulled them out of the crowd to talk to them, Alesha couldn't stop jumping up and down on the spot, all trace of exhaustion and sleeplessness banished in a second.

A clearly impressed Bruce, who had once compared Alesha to a British Beyoncé, told her, 'You could become the biggest female star in this country.' Stunned, the singer mimed, 'What?' Before modestly saying, 'Bruce, you're so funny.'

Dance partner Matthew agreed. 'You are a star in the making,' he said. 'You have worked so hard and given 150 per cent, you could be a professional dancer, and you are a sheer joy to be with.'

'There's only one Beyoncé,' Alesha blushed later. 'When Bruce says that I get embarrassed. It's very sweet . . . but it's not true.'

Matt Di Angelo was magnanimous in defeat: 'Alesha's a great dancer. She really deserves to be here. They've worked so hard and I'm just grateful that the viewers kept me in for this long.'

For the triumphant winner it was 'the best Christmas present a girl could ask for'.

'I'm on cloud nine,' she said. 'I feel so honoured to have been a part of such a fantastic show.'

Later, Alesha admitted that she was convinced she would be runner-up in the final, which was watched by twelve million people. 'I convinced myself and everyone else I wasn't going to win. I thought pretty boy Matt was going to do it. I was ready to fall into Matthew's arms. But in that one moment everything was worth it. It was one of the best feelings in the world.'

Her one regret was that she would not be able to spend so much time with Matthew, with whom she had become incredibly close. 'I nearly cried when I had to leave him. But I sent him a text saying I hope we'll be friends forever. His family say I brought him out of his shell. That's from all my constant talking. I don't shut up.'

The judges were full of praise for their new belle of the ball. 'Alesha Dixon was incredible,' commented Len. 'She's probably the best that there's been, absolutely a fantastic dancer.'

'Alesha was great,' agreed Bruno. 'What is incredible is that I thought the Latin would have been her strength but in fact she was magic in ballroom. You don't expect a sassy, sexy girl to do so well in ballroom. She did a fantastic job, and I was so happy she won. It was very well deserved.'

Craig picked up on her recent past and thought she would be an inspiration to many women. 'Alesha Dixon was a stunning dancer, the best female all-rounder we've had,' he said. 'She's a real inspiration. She's the most wonderful character, the most beautiful person backstage and, onstage, she's a dream. To think that people like that can be treated so badly in their private lives is awful, but it offers hope to those in similar situations because she got herself out of it and has triumphed.

'It's good that they know about that because it encourages people to get themselves out of it too. I don't mean just by going to ballroom dancing lessons, but that's a start because you can meet new people and start feeling good about yourself, because you are doing something for yourself.'

For Matthew Cutler the experience would go down as one of the best in his life. 'Winning *Strictly Come Dancing* was like a dream come true for me,' he said the following year. 'Alesha was amazing; she had the rare balance of dedication, fun and talent. The whole experience was mad, exciting, exhausting – I loved it!'

Alesha had had the time of her life and it was an experience she was never going to forget. 'For four months I felt like a free spirit,' she told *The Observer* a year later. 'Every day I woke up, I had a smile on my face because I would be getting up to go dancing. It was a better experience than I could have ever imagined.

'I used to watch the show with my nan. I remember Zoë Ball dancing the tango and thinking it was the only reality show that I would want to go on.

'I thought I would love all the Latin dances and I thought the waltz would be my least favourite dance, but it turned out to be my favourite. Once you have mastered the steps, you feel like you are just floating on air.

'And dancing with a partner is the nicest way you can dance. It is very romantic. We just don't have that in our culture any more. It makes you feel like a lady.'

A year on from the worst Christmas of her life, when all around her looked bleak and the newspapers were full of her failed marriage, Alesha Dixon was once more a star in the ascendant and the future looked bright.

What better way to get over being dumped than sashaying your way to a sought-after trophy, earning millions of admirers and become the hottest property in the country at the same time?

'It's put a smile on my face,' she said simply. '2007 is great. I thought it was going to be rubbish.'

CHAPTER TWELVE

Does She Clean Up?

'You dance as if your life depended on it,' said Craig Revel Horwood after Alesha's spectacular show dance. To an extent, that's exactly what she was doing. With her tattered solo career and marriage split firmly behind her, the show was the starting block to a new life and was about to open so many doors that she was spinning faster than a Viennese waltz.

'It wasn't until the final night of *Strictly*, after Matthew and I had been declared the winners, that it hit me,' she told the *Daily Mail* later. 'We were asked to go on the dance floor to perform for the very last time and the band played Take That's 'Rule The World'. It's a really magical song, all about destiny.

'Before I did the show, I was nervous it was going to hurt my career because being on a reality TV show is not seen as cool within the music industry. But it was a gamble I had to take. When Matthew picked me up and spun me round during that final dance, I felt that the stars had aligned for me. I knew then that everything was going to be OK.'

Bruce had immediately spotted her potential when he called her 'Britain's Beyoncé', and PR guru Max Clifford predicted she could earn millions in the twelve months after her win, with magazine deals, product endorsement and album sales. And he predicted that she could even cash in on her tough childhood, should she so choose. 'What the win has given her is the biggest shop window she could have wanted,' he said. 'In the next twelve months she will have another load of offers. In time for her next album there will be TV opportunities and advertising opportunities. She's a very attractive girl and, as she's now red-hot, she should have the most amazing year.'

On Christmas Eve, two days after her victory, her agent was inundated with calls and her publicist Liz Matthews commented, 'The world is her oyster. She's the nation's sweetheart.'

'Look at me now,' said Alesha. 'I've learned to dance, I'm happy and I believe it was meant to happen. *Strictly* has just given me a real zest for life. I thrive on hard work, and even though my body is in pain and tired, my first choice is to get up and do something. Life is so short. We should all grasp it.'

First priority for an exhausted Alesha, however, was time to chill out, spend time with her family and enjoy a well-earned rest. And she revealed the gruelling training she endured for the show left her feeling battered and bruised and far from glamorous.

'I was training ten hours a day and my body was simply exhausted,' she revealed in the *News of the World*. 'By the time I got to the final I'd lost a stone. The minute the show ended my body collapsed. I couldn't walk! My feet were killing me and I had to wear Ugg boots to the after party!'

Returning home to the bosom of her family, surrounded by mum, nans, brothers and sisters, Alesha could truly enjoy the festive season, in the knowledge that the previous Christmas had been her lowest point. But instead of her usual Christmas tradition of inviting the family round for a slap-up feast, Alesha was forced to let them do all the work. 'I couldn't leave my chair. I had bruises all over my legs and a strapped knee.'

Unlike most girls, who would revel in the idea of losing a stone and getting fit while being paid for it, Alesha took a good look at her new slimmer frame and didn't like what she saw. 'I lost loads of weight during *Strictly Come Dancing* but I hated being skinny,' she told *Fabulous* magazine later. 'I saw a picture of myself in the gold Julien Macdonald dress I wore at the after-show party and I looked way too thin. That Christmas, I sat in my chair and didn't stop eating.'

Even so, after a few days with her aching feet up, Alesha was ready to celebrate her year. Before the final she had promised, 'I'm going to throw a massive party to look back on what an incredible year this has been. After 2006, I was hoping for a better 2007. But this year has ended better than I could ever have imagined. Roll on 2008.'

On the eve of New Year's Eve, she did just that with a huge bash at the trendy Kenza Club in London, where celebrity pals Matt Di Angelo, Flavia Cacace, Matthew Cutler and Brendan Cole got the chance to strut their stuff on the dance floor while Alesha kept her still blistered feet snug in her Uggs.

By 8 January she was once again up and running – literally. The superfit singer donned her trainers to join Johnny Vaughan in London's Leicester Square to promote a charity run for Capital Radio's Help a London Child appeal. The aim was to raise £250,000 for the charity by encouraging people to take part in the BUPA 10K run in July 2008, and Alesha pledged to run herself on the day. 'It doesn't matter if you're an experienced runner or a complete novice, you can skip, jump or walk your way around the route if you like. You can be sure to have a great time while raising money for a very worthy cause.'

It wasn't long before she was throwing herself into work again either. After a welcome rest, the bubbly beauty was off to Japan to promote *Fired Up,* the album that Polydor had refused to release in the UK. Japan had been Mis-Teeq's biggest selling territory outside the UK, and Alesha, who had held on to the rights to the tracks, persuaded the Japanese record label that had released Mis-Teeq's albums, to take a chance on this one.

On the way, she treated herself to a ten-day stopover in Thailand to visit dad Melvin. 'My dad moved to Thailand because he loves the country,' she said. 'I hope that we get close, it's an ideal opportunity because I am going to Japan for work so it's on the way.'

The gamble paid off and 'Lipstick', the first single, went to number one in ringtones! 'They loved it,' said a delighted Alesha. 'They put "Lipstick" out and the ringtone sold so many it was number one. They don't have a singles chart out there, so the ringtone is their equivalent.

'In Japan, they always say to me, "Ah, you have such a small head!" Apparently that's a compliment! Su-Elise and Sabrina used to call me "peahead".'

Travel was broadening her horizons all the time and she had even picked up the odd bit of Japanese. 'Japanese fans buy you a lot of Hello Kitty stuff. They're so polite. I've learned how to say, "Hello, my name's Alesha," and, "How are you?" I can count to four on stage and I can also order a beef dinner.'

Because of the promotional visit, Alesha was forced to turn down the *Strictly Come Dancing* live tour, which runner-up Matt Di Angelo and pal Letitia Dean took part in. Instead, she began to look at new projects and concentrated on working on her next solo album with Xenomania hitmaker Brian Higgins. And before *Strictly* had finished, a bidding war to get her signed up to a record label for the album had already started. Ironically, one of the names on the table was Polydor, the very company who had dumped her in the first place.

In the meantime, Alesha landed a lucrative ad for car company Ford. Looking classy in a floor-length evening gown, she sings the seductive ballad '4 U I Will', including the lines, 'My love you're adorable,' and, 'When we're apart I dream of you,' to a Ford Focus with the number plate 'ALESHA'. The instruments accompanying her were made entirely from car parts.

Despite her millions of male admirers, however, that was as close as Alesha was getting to a real romance at the time. 'I'm not actively looking for someone, but I am dating and I feel like if I meet someone, then that would be cool,' she told the *Sunday Mirror*. 'I turn thirty next year and when I was in my early twenties I thought that by that age you'd have to have children and be doing certain things with your life. But I don't feel that pressure any more. Your twenties used to be the years you lived your life, but I'm starting to feel that thirty to thirty-five will be another amazing chapter, so I'm just going to go with the flow and see where life takes me.'

Joking that her ideal man would be a chef, so she could be seduced with food, she was serious about not rushing into a relationship. She also delivered a subtle sideswipe at cheating ex Harvey. 'Obviously, dating changes as you get older, and the way I'd want to meet someone now is completely different to how I went about it when I was twenty-two. I'm a bit more cautious about men now. I can't deal with lies. These days I feel I'd want to meet someone and get to know them as a friend first rather than go out to try to find a man. Unfortunately you have to go out if you want to meet a man – and doing *Strictly* means I haven't been out for about three months.'

But in an interview in *FHM*, some time later, she admitted that all that raunchy dancing had left her in a naughty mood. 'I'll tell you a secret. Most people on *Strictly Come Dancing* are really horny all the time. Imagine you're being groped for five hours a day, hips rubbing together, hands everywhere . . . it's like foreplay, but no actual sex. You're not getting any punani at the end!'

As a single lady, she said, she had to settle for 'a cold shower and a cup of hot chocolate before bed'. Despite her early nights alone, she found the time to encourage others to behave sensibly, putting her weight behind a Department of Health Valentine's Day campaign to promote safe sex. To get the point across she posed naked in a bath full of condoms for the Condom Essential War Campaign. 'Using a condom is about being confident enough to look after yourself,' she informed the nation. 'You shouldn't rely on the other person to have one – if you carry a condom you'll always be prepared, safe and in control.'

There may have been no man in her life, but on the work front she had plenty to keep her busy. As someone who had always had forthright views on the world and a desire to use her skills for the good of others wherever possible, Alesha was keen to use her new high profile to highlight some issues close to her heart. Having been a cover girl on many a magazine, she launched a campaign against airbrushing and fake body images in the media, and the BBC were right behind her. In February, they announced that she would front a sixty-minute documentary called *Look But Don't Touch*, which would explore the issues surrounding the portrayal of beauty in today's society. Danny Cohen, the controller of BBC3, explained, 'This is a subject she feels strongly about, and I'm sure she will make a passionate and thought-provoking documentary. Alesha will undertake a personal journey in the programme to explore what it means to be beautiful in Britain today.'

In the making of the programme, Alesha approached various magazines to see if anyone was willing to put her on the cover, unadulterated and unbrushed. She also talked to young women and children about the affect that magazine images have on their own perception of themselves, and even talked to one playschool child who stated that 'size 14 is too big'.

'Generally, women think about how they look and their image every day,' she said. 'Personally I've found that, as I've got older, I've become more accepting of my body and see it for what it is. I'm far less worried nowadays.'

Alesha also met the parents of a teenager who had paid thousands for their daughter's breast enhancement. 'As part of the show I watched this girl have a boob job and it was horrific!' she recalled. 'But I was happy for her because she'd been bullied for being flat-chested. If I was her parent it would be a hard situation. You might be against plastic surgery but you want your daughter to be happy.'

The show, which was aired in July 2008, set the worried warbler thinking about body image and how women in the spotlight can have an affect on young, impressionable girls. Naturally slim, although she had never been a follower of diets herself, Alesha revealed a shocking secret. 'I don't diet. Never have,' she insisted. I think food is there to be enjoyed, so I eat what I want, when I want. I'm a healthy eater anyway, but if I want to eat a packet of Minstrels or a couple of Oreos, I'll happily do it. When I became a solo artist, someone at the record label asked my manager to have a word with me because I was "looking a bit heavy on TV". I only found out later. Making normal girls think they're overweight is disgusting. I say just be yourself. Whatever your natural body shape is, then that's OK. There's no right or wrong way to look – we should celebrate women just as they are. Food's one of the great things in life.'

Food is a subject close to her heart. Despite her perfect curves, regained through eating normally after her *Strictly* weight loss, Alesha genuinely eats whatever she wants and loves everything from exotic meals to a good old-fashioned Sunday roast. Growing up with a Jamaican father and an English mother has left her with adventurous taste and a love of her dad's family's native food.

'I love anything Jamaican,' she has said. 'Particularly salt fish and goat curry. But last Sunday I had a good old roast dinner, I had extra potatoes, and then I cleared up everybody's leftover potatoes too – I'm like the family food dustbin. I prefer to have a bit of meat on me,' she explains. 'Besides, everyone who knows me will tell you I just love my food too much. Me, sacrifice food for a washboard stomach? Never!'

Although Alesha's legs were an impressive sight throughout the previous autumn's events, she admits that she detests her feet, and never wears strappy sandals or flip flops. 'I never get my feet out,' she revealed in the *Daily Mirror*. 'I had an operation on my foot a few years ago to straighten a bone and it left a huge scar.'

She did concede that the best part of her body was indeed the long shapely legs which carried her through the competition and garnered a few more male viewers for the show. 'They're long and I like the shape of them. They're the one part of my body I don't give myself a hard time about. My legs are the sexiest part of my body and have been very good to me. I always show them on a night out.'

While some men were drooling over her perfect pins, others were seeing a business opportunity, and by July she was signed up as the new face – or legs – of hair removal system Veet.

By the summer, everything was going to plan. She had spent some time in LA recording her new album, and was about to meet powerful music producers in Las Vegas. Her documentary was screened on 8 July, to a largely positive response, and she was hoping to set up her own TV production company.

'I want to own the rights to my own show. I'm not a silly girl. It's about empowering myself and having control over what I do,' she told *What's on TV*. 'I'd love to have my own show, which was able to explore many different issues from domestic violence to homelessness to anorexia. You can't change the world with a documentary but you can raise debate.'

In July, at the International Motor Show at Londons ExCel, where she was launching Ford's new model Zetec S, she beamed, 'I've just set up a TV production company, White Bear Productions, and we're developing ideas at the minute. My potential dream and goal is to have my own show. It would be a fun show but with a theme running through it that tackles and looks at different social issues. We've started filming a fly-on-the-wall documentary that's going to go through my production company, which won't come out until 2009. It'll be following my journey, making the album and what happens when the album comes out. Then we're looking at little one-off documentaries that cover different social issues because that is something I'm interested in. I like to get out there with people and do things, question things, bring awareness to things, and if

I'm in a position to do that, I think, "Why not? I'm going to try to do it."'

In the meantime, she strengthened her position as articulate spokesperson for youth issues by appearing on the hard-hitting political programme *This Week*, hosted by Andrew Neil. As well as discussing her views on a number of issues with politicians Michael Portillo and Diane Abbott, she provided a lighter note by waltzing with then acting Liberal Democrat leader Vince Cable.

By that time she had also signed a four-album deal with Asylum Records, a division of Atlantic Records, which was behind such hits as Ironik's 'Stay With Me' and Wiley's 'Wearing My Rolex'. Showing her smart business sense she had retained the rights to the tracks she had worked on at Polydor and urged young musicians to follow her example. 'It's really important you take ownership of things and that you don't hastily sign contracts you're not sure about, because you can get really screwed over,' she advised.

The deal covered more than her music. Asylum Records would also be involved in other aspects of her career, including touring, merchandise and sponsorship, working with Alesha's manager Malcolm Blair. 'Alesha is a highly accomplished artist and performer and we are thrilled to welcome her to Asylum UK,' commented Ben Cook, the company's managing director. 'Her planned collaborations with cutting-edge producers such as Xenomania promise some world-class, credible, contemporary pop.'

The newly relaunched label had been placed under the auspices of Cook, who had previously headed up the underground Ministry of Sound label, and was at the forefront of grime, garage and R&B music. Alesha was clearly impressed with their proposals and, despite having several bids from more mainstream and powerful labels on the table, she was happy with her choice.

'Asylum Records are hungry and they are going to work hard,' she remarked. 'They believe in me and the ideas are flowing out. The way the album is shaping up – things really couldn't be better.'

And she revealed that, when Polydor had dropped her in 2006, her natural optimism had shone through in her darkest hour. 'When Polydor dropped me, at that point, as an artist, I didn't know whether I would be signed by another major label,' she admitted. 'But deep down in my heart I believed that I would – even though I was upset.'

She also revealed the thinking behind the shock move from the record label and her surprise that they even released the second single. 'I'd spent a year and a half making it so it was a huge setback. The label dropped me just before the second single, "Knockdown", came out, so I don't know why they released that. "Knockdown" wasn't getting played on the radio, the first single had only got to number 14 and the label decided they didn't want to release the album without a big hit. I understand that but it was heartbreaking.'

The thing that amazed Alesha most was the sudden clamour from record companies to sign her when just a year earlier some of them wouldn't even take her calls. The newfound interest pre-empted the plan to finish the album before signing. 'Life after the show was great,' she said later. 'I had all these labels coming to me.

'My plan was to make an album then go to labels, now they were queuing up to sign me. It was a dream come true.'

In October, Alesha was at the biggest MOBO award cere-mony ever, held at London's Wembley Arena, where she presented the Best Male award to Dizzee Rascal. She attended with her old girlband pal Su-Elise which, inevitably, got tongues wagging about a Mis-Teeq reunion.

'People kept coming up to us and asking if Mis-Teeq would get back together,' she said. 'I don't know, because we're all doing out own thing, but maybe one day we will get together and do a one-off show. Su-Elise has opened up her own stage school, and she's doing really well. Sabrina is still recording and it's still her dream to be a singer. She's working on new mate-rial and I really wish her well, I hope she brings something out in 2009.'

With her thirtieth birthday fast approaching, Alesha was sur-rounded by the latest up-and-coming acts, such as Tinchy Stryder, Jay Sean and Flo Rida. But she was delighted that Estelle, who had been through a similar record company let-down to her own, picked up two awards for Best Song ('American Boy') and Best Female. 'I think the MOBOs is something that is definitely worth supporting,' Alesha said. 'It was a great night and I got to catch up with some old friends. I felt a bit old, though, because there are all these new people coming through. It was great to see Estelle clean up because she got dropped in this country and went out to the States and made it happen. So great to see her get the respect she deserves.'

The night ended badly for Alesha and co, however, when the goody bags packed with expensive items went missing from the boot of their car. She took it on the chin with a grin. 'Fair play to them, they got some good stuff. There was a mobile phone, a watch and all sorts.'

By now the dynamic diva had her fingers in so many pies she was working constantly, and she wouldn't have it any other way. 'I'm an active person, you'll never catch me resting.'

As Max Clifford had predicted after Alesha had twirled off with the *Strictly* trophy, she was the hottest property in music and TV and she was revelling in her moment. 'I've got all these opportunities,' she continued. 'It's so empowering.'

On the romantic front, in March and April there were reports of a string of dates with Aston Villa footballer John Carew. Soccer's nice guy, renowned for his charity work and caring nature off the pitch, Carew seemed a perfect fit and was happy to take it slow, which suited Alesha.

'First of all we'll be friends and then we'll see what the future holds but we've spent some time with each other,' he admitted in the *Daily Mail* in April. 'I wouldn't say we're a couple because we are still getting to know each other but she's a fantastic person. And I know all about her dancing, she's great and she helps me with my footwork.'

The relationship sadly didn't work out, although the pair remained friends. Alesha was still 'Holding Out For A Hero'. 'I want to meet somebody special. But at the moment I'm working every day – I don't know when I'm supposed to meet somebody! I'm waiting to be swept away on a white horse. By the time I'm fifty I'd like to have achieved all I can in music, maybe done a few films and had my own TV show. Then I'd like to be able to relax and chill out with the people I love.'

And, as always, she attributed her success to the person she loves most – her mum. 'She's the reason why I'm able to do what I'm doing now – she supported me.'

CHAPTER THIRTEEN

Years Roll On

Reaching a thirtieth birthday is a milestone in anyone's life, but for a single, childless woman who has set her heart on a family by the time she is thirty-five, it can hit even harder. Not, however, if you are the ever effervescent Alesha Dixon. Not even the prospect of another decade passing could get her down.

As the October date loomed, she looked and felt better than she ever had before and she was having too much fun to care about entering her fourth decade. 'Getting older doesn't bother me. I'll be thirty in October and I'm looking forward to it. I still feel as young as I did in my early twenties, but now I have a wiser head on my shoulders,' she said in the News of the World.

'When I was young my dad wouldn't let me leave the house without moisturizing, because black skin can look a bit grey otherwise. I'm still obsessive about it . . . I don't like the idea of cosmetic surgery. I would like to think that when I get wrinkles I will embrace the changes, rather than see them as a flaw.'

But she admitted that she would never rule out cosmetic surgery in the distant future. 'That's tricky,' she reasoned. 'The one thing you don't want to be is a hypocrite because our opinions change as the years pass. Right now, no. But it's like my mum says: until you look in the mirror and see wrinkles or something that's dropped, you don't know how you will feel.'

Now that she was a familiar face on ads and magazine covers, fans were clamouring for her beauty tips. Alesha was happy to share and, typically, her best tip was: stay happy. 'My mum's advice is: "If you're happy on the inside you will always look beautiful – so do things that make you happy!"'

On a more practical note she advised, 'It's an inexpensive trick but always pluck and shape your eyebrows. They really frame your face. If you find someone who does threading, it lasts for ages.'

She also revealed her obsession for lip gloss, of which she had over twenty varieties, in different shades of pink, and said she loved creams from the luxury cosmetic range Bobbi Brown. Her favourite perfume is Flowerbomb, from Viktor and Rolf, and she said the constant use of make-up for her line of work meant it was necessary to treat herself to regular facials.

While she was happy with her legs, she admitted she was hoping to grow bigger in the bust and rear when she got older. 'I burn off lots of energy. But my body may change as I get older,' she told *FHM*. 'My Jamaican nan has massive gazungas that sit on her belt. She's a proper West Indian woman. I hope I get her boobs. And a nice arse that sticks out and isn't just a flat extension of my back. Maybe I should eat more Jamaican food. I love curried goat and jerk chicken and pig's tail.'

Even her fashion sense had matured. Gone were the dodgy hairstyles and denim minis of the Mis-Teeq days. On the rare occasions Alesha ventured out, simple classy style was more up her street.

She was happy to look back and laugh at her own image, especially in the video for 'B With Me', which was played back to her on Justin Lee Collins' chat show. 'What was with the blonde hair?' she laughed. 'That blonde weave was just wrong! And so was the denim outfit! Oh, the things you do in your twenties!' She also called her multicoloured hair in the 'One Night Stand' video 'hilarious'.

Alesha's early twenties had been dominated by hard work and ambition, as she and Mis-Teeq struggled for success and put their all into making their mark on the world. Her late twenties were remembered more for the turmoil of her personal and professional life than for her music. Not surprisingly, she was quite pleased to see the back of that decade, even though it had ultimately ended in jubilation.

'Getting older does not bother me. I don't feel any different and I have just as much energy, so I am embracing my age,' she told *The Mail on Sunday*. 'My twenties were a big roller coaster packed with ups and downs, so I hope life will even out a bit for the next decade. It is all about your state of mind and women have proved that thirty is the start of a lot of new things. People have kids later and find success in their careers in their thirties and forties. Things have changed, perceptions have changed. I don't think age is a big deal any more. In my twenties I was still learning about life and about myself. Now I feel ready to start a new adventure with a wiser head on my shoulders. I would hate to go back and do it all again. I am much happier where I am. Life looks good and this birthday is a new beginning for me.'

Her innate wisdom had clearly grown stronger over the years and she was brimming with philosophy about the 'good place' she had found herself in. 'I've got to a point now where I'm beginning to feel fearless,' she revealed. 'I don't have the anxieties that I had in my early twenties – the normal worries you have when you first go out into the big bad world. If you have a positive frame of mind, you can manifest positive things in your life.'

'I'm more comfortable in my skin now than I was in my twenties, and I feel much wiser,' she told *Cosmopolitan*. 'I'm positive about the future. I used to worry about it, but I've learnt that worrying is a waste of energy because it doesn't actually change anything. Now I accept things as they are and live for today, whereas before I was always looking ahead. I feel stronger because of things that have happened to me. In a weird way they've helped me.'

Ex-husband Harvey and partner Javine, who were still living together in London, now had a baby. The reality show runner-up gave birth to baby Angel in February 2008, commenting that Harvey is 'going to be amazing, the best dad in the world'.

At the same time many of Alesha's closest friends had settled down and started families of their own and there were moments in her busy life when she longed for that lifestyle. At other times she reflected how fortunate she was with her life and once again pushed the thought of babies to the back of her mind as something she would do in the future.

'I'd love to have kids one day,' she said. 'All of my friends have got children – in fact most of them are on their third – so there are times when I do feel a bit left out. I look at their lives and think they've got lovely family set-ups. I'd admire that and then there's that little girl in me that wanted to have a baby at the same time as my friends so the kids could all play together. But my friends say they envy aspects of my life too, so it's a case of thinking that the grass is always greener. And so many women are having children in their thirties and even forties now that I'm not worried. It used to worry me, but not any more.'

Harvey was another subject that had been pushed to the back of her mind, in his case permanently. 'All I can say is I have moved on and am in such a different place now,' she insisted. 'I am happy. Things are great and I am very excited about my new album. Anything is possible for me now. I am single but I have not been put off relationships. I was always taught not to tarnish everyone with the same brush so I try to be that kind of person. I never take baggage from the past into a new relationship; I learn from it and hope it helps.'

And in *The Mail on Sunday* she reiterated that the joy of *Strictly* and the support of the public had made a huge difference in helping her pick up the pieces and carry on. 'That helped me in the sense that I felt people were on my side,' she said. 'When I watch the old shows on tape it looks like I am having the best time – and I am – because I was conscious the public were willing me to do well. I thank everyone who comes up to me and tells me that they voted for me. I mean it because they don't realize what a part they played in the next chapter of my life. Why me? I don't know. For whatever reason, they supported me. The show lifted my spirits and gave me something to do every day that made me smile and brought me joy. It was great to know I wasn't going through things alone. There is no greater feeling than knowing people are wishing you well. I can't imagine how it must feel to be on the other side of that and have everyone against you.'

With her burgeoning career on TV panning out nicely, and a new album about to be released, the singer had everything she could wish for as she celebrated her thirtieth – well, almost everything. 'Come on guys – it's my thirtieth,' she joked in one tabloid. 'Somebody has to be there for me surely. I was sitting in my house last night and my cousin was upstairs with her boyfriend – and I was jealous!'

At the same time, Alesha is not one to rush in to anything and was keen to take any new relationship at her own pace. 'You can't be with someone for six years and, after a year, be ready to put your heart on the line again. I don't do things by halves,' she said.

Although, she had been busy, work-wise, in the year since claiming the *Strictly* title, Alesha was seldom seen on the red carpets in London, or the trendy nightspots where the public and journalists hang out to play 'spot the celebrity'. Many were surprised she was lying so low as her star was shining so bright.

'I was making my album, which I'd started recording before I went on *Strictly*,' she explained in *The Observer*. 'And at the end of the day it's not my job to turn up at premieres. I get quite embarrassed at those kinds of things; they're not important to me. Some people worry when they're not in the tabloids but I'd rather just be seen when I'm doing something constructive. I don't have a desire to be seen all the time. If I've got an album, I'm doing *Strictly* or I've got a documentary on TV, that's fine. The problem with young girls now is that they aspire to be famous, rather than to be well known for being good at something. Having said that, my goddaughter wants me to take her to the *High School Musical 3* premiere, so you might see me on the red carpet for that!'

Strangely enough, this star-studded event, which saw teen idols Zac Efron, Vanessa Hudgens and Ashley Tisdale wow a large crowd of screaming girls in London's Leicester Square, fell on the evening of Alesha's actual birthday, 7 October 2008. But you can't let an excited goddaughter down, so the birthday girl kicked off celebrations in a temperate style by walking down the red carpet and watching the box-office-busting movie. She made up for it later, however, when she and a group of girls headed for heaving hotspot Bungalow 8 and, afterwards, stayed above the club at the St Martin's Hotel.

It seems like a good time was had by all. Not only was she spotted outside the club in her dressing gown in the early hours of the morning, but she admitted later that the most 'scandalous' thing she had done was 'flashing my girlfriends in a lift on my thirtieth birthday'.

Her millions of fans were not missing out on the celebrations either. Through a fan website and a showbiz gossip site, they submitted pictures and messages for a special fan book and money to go towards a beautiful jewellery box inscribed with the message 'Happy Birthday, Alesha'. The singer was deeply touched, submitting, in return, a thank you video in which she told them, 'Thank you so much for my lovely, lovely presents. Some of the drawings were amazing, the messages were fantastic. I called up Matthew and told him all about it because I was so touched by it. It brought back some great memories for me and it was one of the best birthday presents I've ever, ever had. There were even photographs in there that I'd never seen. It was a lovely surprise. Thank you all so much for your support. Can't wait to see you all soon. Love you guys.'

Despite the fact that 'My friends keep ringing me up to tell me how it's all over!' Alesha vowed that thirty would be another turning point and that she would not be resting on her laurels. 'It's important that I keep growing and challenging myself,' she remarked to *Cosmopolitan*. 'When I get to seventy, I want to be able to look back and know I took life by the scruff of the neck and went for it. I'm never going to look back and think, "If only". Plus, I believe that if something isn't meant for you, it won't come to you. I've accepted that now and, as a result, I'm changing my attitude to life.'

'I'm planning to live until I'm a hundred, so middle age is a long way off,' she told *Metro*. 'I've still got my legs and I'm all intact. I've got as much energy as I had when I was twenty-five.'

With pop careers and celebrity spotlights being notoriously transient, Alesha was asked where she saw herself ten years on. 'I'll be forty, so maybe I'll be drowning my sorrows with a bottle of vodka!' she joked. 'I'd like to still be working but be more chilled out. I pray to God that I'll be in a good place and that I'll be optimistic about turning fifty. And I like to think I'll have a family.'

CHAPTER FOURTEEN

The Alesha Show

Exactly two years after Harvey's affair with Javine broke in the tabloids, Alesha's rise from the ashes was complete. Her album, *The Alesha Show*, was about to hit the shops and the first single 'The Boy Does Nothing' was released on 10 November 2008.

Clearly influenced by her new love of Latin dancing, the single, written with Brian Higgins, had a racy Mambo beat and an impossibly catchy chorus. The lyrics, which blasted a fictional boyfriend for not being able to dance – or do anything much of any use at all – were definitely not referring to her housework-loving, So Solid rapper ex: 'Does he wash up? No, he never wash up. Does he clean up? No, he never clean up,' she warbles, before issuing a warning to all potential suitors about 'a man with two left feet', singing, 'And if the man can't dance, he gets no second chance.'

Her experience in the capable hands of dance teacher Matthew Cutler was palpable too as she urged everyone to Mambo, singing, 'I wanna see you move your body in turn. I wanna see you shake your hips and learn.'

'It was actually written before I went on *Strictly*,' said Alesha. 'When I came out of it, though, I had all this fresh impetus, so we speeded it up.'

The video, directed by Michael Gracey, the talented art director from the film *Moulin Rouge*, had echoes of the burlesque as Alesha and a troop of female dancers wore super-short *Strictly*-style dresses to shimmy and shake their way through a frenetic routine in a dimly lit theatre. The performance could well have been choreographed by her former dance partner, with many of the rapid Latin steps she had learned in their intensive training put to good use.

'It was two days of solid dancing,' she revealed. '*Strictly* helps you become more conscious of what you're doing with your arms. I do a little cha-cha-cha in the video, and showed it to some dancers from *Strictly*. They all said it looked good but I think they were being polite!'

The sexy sirens in the video, and their close interaction with each other, apparently came as something of a surprise to Alesha. 'When I was told I'd be getting up close and personal with six dancers for the video I didn't realize they meant girls rather than guys! . . . But I had a lot of fun as the choreography was so cheeky and flirty.'

With a message encouraging people to dance, it was the perfect follow-up to her previous year's triumph and tapped into the fan base that watched her become the queen of ballroom every Saturday night. The track, she asserted, was a perfect antidote to the crippling credit crunch the UK and the world were experiencing. 'Dancing costs nothing,' she said. 'It's recession-proof! We need a good feelgood song now, what with everything going on in the world.'

The track was also something of a surprise to the music press, who were expecting more of an R&B Beyoncé-style sound. 'People might look at me and see a mixed-race girl and think, "Oh, she'll do R&B," but I grew up in a predominantly white area in Great Britain, my father's Jamaican and my mother listened to Pink Floyd,' she told *The Observer*. 'I feel like I've got a nice mix. As for the "Mambo No.5" sound, it just feels right. The song started over as more jazzy, bluesy music, but it ended up going there.'

In October she took a short break from promoting the single to pick up the National Television Award for the Most Popular Entertainment Show on behalf of *Strictly Come Dancing*, delighting in the fact that it beat both *The X Factor* and *Britain's Got Talent*. Simon Cowell, who fronts both shows, was in the audience and was not pleased. 'His face was a picture,' she laughed afterwards. 'Oh my God. It was better than actually winning!'

In the month before the single was released Alesha appeared on numerous TV shows to perform live, including *Loose Women*, *GMTV* and, of course, *Strictly Come Dancing*. There she sang as she danced with professionals, including Flavia Cacace, Vincent Simone and Kristina Rihanoff, and she finished by fulfilling her wish to dance with Matthew Cutler once again.

After the leaked video for the song was posted on a clip-sharing site, getting over 200,000 viewings in twenty-four hours, it seemed Alesha had a sure-fire hit on her hands. In fact, in one week it jumped seventy-six places on the UK charts from number 84 to number 8 on downloads alone. The following week it reached 5, making it her first solo top-ten single. It also shot up the charts across Europe, reaching the number 2 spot in Spain, Finland and France.

'First off, I'm very, very, very, very excited about the chart position this week!' blogged Alesha on her fan site. 'When I found out it was number 5, I was over the moon! A massive thank you to everyone that bought it – I've been completely blown away! It's really amazing because you think that only you care because it's your project but other people out there care just as much. Some people have sent me messages saying they've bought it seven times! Thank you so much!'

'On Saturday night I went out for my best friend's thirtieth birthday dinner and the DJ decided to play "The Boy Does Nothing" – it was really embarrassing! He tried to get me to go up onstage but I sort of hid in the corner and watched everyone else dance. The whole place formed this circle and took it in turns dancing in the middle like that scene at the end of the video.'

She also revealed she was in agony, once more, through too much dancing. She had been in the States filming the video for the next single, 'Breathe Slow', and had a neck injury. 'Right now I'm currently sitting here in pain!' she blogged. 'I've done so much dancing in preparation for the 'Breathe Slow' video shoot in Las Vegas and I've done my neck in from swinging it about so much, I had to go and buy loads of Deep Heat – there's only so much the body can take before it collapses! There's so much to learn for the video – but you have to go through these pain barriers sometimes to get the results you want. Hopefully it's going to be amazing!'

The huge success of the single paved the way for the long-awaited album, *The Alesha Show*, released just two weeks later on 24 November. The fact that the album got off the ground even before her *Strictly* fame was largely down to Xenomania genius Brian Higgins, who had the courage to reach out a hand to the broken singer during her worst time.

'The belief that he had in me, when someone of that calibre reaches out to you when the chips are down: that spoke volumes to me,' she said in *The Daily Telegraph*. 'We were just going to write songs without a contract and then see what we could do with it.'

As streetwise as she is talented, Alesha was aware that the success of the album could be determined by those around her as much as her own input. As well as Xenomania, collaborations included Duffy's co-writer and producer Steve Brooker and American R&B producers The Underdogs. 'I like lots of different things and I'm very open-minded when it comes to music,' she told Dermot O'Leary on Radio 2. 'Obviously "The Boy Does Nothing" is very pop, very bold and in your face, but as the album progresses you'll see a more serious side. There's some guitar-based tracks, some emotional songs, so it's broader. A lot of people like a bit of everything so I've tried to make an album that reflects that.'

The influence of the various hitmakers on the tracks was clear, as was the effect her *Strictly* win had on the tone of the music. The catchy mainstream tunes and smoky-voiced ballads were some way from her underground beginnings and designed to appeal to her new fan base, whose ages ranged from tots to pensioners.

The programme, she said, 'had the biggest impact imaginable. Even though Mis-Teeq were successful, a lot of people did not know who we were. *Strictly* opened up this whole new demographic, which was quite scary at first. I was getting letters from people as young as four and as old as eighty. So many people would approach me and I was just not used to that. I had to adjust and it changed my approach to the new record. I had to make a less targeted album with songs that young and old could like.'

On a chat show in May 2009, she denied she had intended to boost her flagging career by joining *Strictly Come Dancing*, and said her feelings were that it would have the opposite effect. 'I really wanted to do the show but I was nervous about doing it because I'd started making the album,' she told host Justin Lee Collins. 'I think there's this preconceived idea that people do reality shows to kick-start their careers, but I was actually worried that it would affect it, because in the music industry there is a bit of snobbery with artists who do reality shows. But I was a massive fan of the show. And I never went to stage school or had dance classes when I was growing up. I really wanted to be taught by professionals. So I followed my instincts and have no regrets. It turned out even better than I imagined.'

Being a co-writer on all the songs on *The Alesha Show*, it would have been a shock if the lyrics didn't reflect at least a little of the pain that she had endured two years earlier. As every songwriter knows, heartbreak can lead to some of the most creative periods of your life and Alesha was bound to pour some of that pain into the album. If nothing else, she was clever enough to know that her fans would be disappointed if the songs didn't reflect her inner feelings.

Sure enough, the familiar chord of painful break-ups does resonate through the album with one particular song, 'Can I Begin?', addressing the loss of her former life with Harvey and her record deal head on. 'There are a few songs on the album which deal with it – that point when I felt like my life had ended after I lost my husband and record deal within two weeks,' she revealed. 'There's one song called "Can I Begin?" which is about making a fresh start and moving forward. It ends on a positive note.'

Avoiding the obvious sullen, self-pitying love song, the track has a reasonably up-tempo beat as she sings about the pain of going through a break-up. But the song follows the story to its more positive conclusion, referring to Alesha's jubilant rebirth as she makes the decision to 'just move on' and put the past behind her. The message was clear; it was a bad time, she had been badly wounded, but she was over it. 'I'm not sitting here hurting,' she said. 'It's the past.'

'I wouldn't have been able to do this album two years ago because the things that I've gone through over the last couple of years have helped shape it,' she observed in an interview with Dermot O'Leary on Radio 2. 'A lot of people say that writing an album is like writing a diary, and I used to say that in Mis-Teeq without really knowing what it meant. But I feel that some of the songs on this album have been a really nice release, a way of getting things out, and hopefully that's when the audience will connect with you because they know you are singing about things that are the truth, and it's coming from an honest place.

'As an artist you write from experience, and draw from life experiences. That's the only way I know how to write so I hope there's a nice balance of feel-good records from where I am now – because I'm in a great place, everything is exciting – but there are tracks on there that reflect what I've been through as well.'

Looking back to two years earlier, and her public split with Harvey, she revealed that the media spotlight was one of the hardest things she had to endure. As an artist who had kept herself out of the headlines on purpose and focussed on her work, she struggled to cope with the paparazzi being camped outside her front door and following her every move.

'Looking back that was one of the things that upset me the most because I'd tried for so long to be very professional, do my job, go home,' she told Dermot O'Leary. 'We were quite sensible girls and the media probably found us quite boring because we weren't controversial. But you have to deal with these things, there's nothing that can be thrown at me now that I can't deal with. It's made me a stronger person and I'm a very happy lady right now.'

Explaining the title of the album Alesha remarked, 'I wrote a song out in France called "The Alesha Show" and it just made sense because I wanted it to be an event, a concept to buy into. For me, this is the entertainment industry, so it's about putting on a show.'

Reviews of the album were mixed, with *The Times* calling it, 'A restless scamper through feisty R&B, 1960s soul, big-band swing and misty-eyed balladry, *The Alesha Show* has as many collaborators as it does styles. The first half, with the groovy "Let's Get Excited" and the tongue-in-cheek, mambo style "The Boy Does Nothing", is great fun. But the "killer" love song turns out to be a damp squib, while the Euro-funk filler "Ooh Baby I Like it Like That" is just as inane as its name.'

Ally Carnworth of *The Observer* commented that while her story was 'the stuff of hitmakers' dreams', it was 'odd then that the top-name producers drafted in to sprinkle stardust on the *Strictly Come Dancing* winner's comeback couldn't have mustered some better tunes. Mambo-tinged current single "The Boy Does Nothing" is infectious enough, but sounds lacklustre by the standards of its creators, Xenomania. And though the kittenish R&B of "Italians Do It Better" and empowerment ballad "Can

I Begin?" are functional, nothing here possesses half the sass and sparkle of the best manufactured pop.'

As the promotion surrounding the album reached fever pitch in November, the worn-out singer was forced to cancel a trip to Thailand, where she had hoped to rest and spend time with her dad. Instead, she chose to put as much work into selling her solo debut as she possibly could. 'If it doesn't work, I want to be completely accountable,' she explained. 'Nothing scares me any more. I've proved to myself that I can get out of bad situations, that I can go through bad times and come out the other end better. I feel I had to take a low, because in Mis-Teeq, although it was hard work, we never had any major obstacles. I'm stronger, I can deal with it, I'm fearless again. There's nothing you could throw at me that I couldn't get through. It's all happened.'

Her packed schedule wasn't all talk of *The Alesha Show*. As well as filming the *Strictly Come Dancing* Christmas Special, where she would perform a Viennese waltz with partner Matthew Cutler to the strains of 'White Christmas', her political ambitions had led her all the way to Downing Street.

Gordon Brown dubbed her a 'national treasure' and, on 6 November, the inspirational singer was invited to attend a reception with Sarah Brown to honour the winners of the *Cosmopolitan* Ultimate Women of the Year Awards. Other stars in attendance at the famous address included *Sex and the City's* Kim Cattrall and the Sugababes.

There, she spent ten minutes talking to the Prime Minister and, a week later, she received a call from Sarah asking her to perform at a charity do at the end of November. Impressed by the singer himself, Gordon, the son of a Church of Scotland minister, decided to drop in on the event for ten minutes while Alesha sang, so she cheekily chose the 1968 Dusty Springfield classic, 'Son Of A Preacher Man'.

'I did the song on Dermot O'Leary's radio show and my manager rang me and said, "Gordon's the son of a preacher so you should definitely do that song for him."' After dedicating the song to him, she followed up with her single, 'The Boy Does Nothing', which she dedicated to his political opponent, Tory leader David Cameron. 'The Prime Minister asked me, "What are you going to be doing next?" I said, "I'm thinking of going into politics – so if you ever need me."'

She even admitted to finding him a tiny bit attractive. 'It may be a shock but I met him recently and that Scottish brogue is far sexier than you may think. He has a twinkle in his eye too.'

Getting into politics was an idea that Alesha was increasingly warming to. After joking that she couldn't wait to get her 'little foot into Downing Street', she appeared on the controversial Nick Ferrari show on LBC radio, where she was thrilled that she got to talk about such issues as Jonathan Ross's suspension from the BBC and multiculturalism. 'It's the only programme I've ever asked my radio plugger to get me on,' she said. 'It was great. You do so many interviews about trivial things, but with this, I got to talk about Jonathan Ross and Russell Brand. I got to talk about multiculturalism. I got to talk about politics.'

With offers still flooding in for her to present and appear on various TV and radio programmes, Alesha's choices even sur-prised those who had been helping steer her career thus far, such as straight-talking Scottish manager Malcolm Blair.

'My manager said, "When you started talking about *Question Time*, I nearly choked on my cornflakes."'

But Alesha, who said she was offered jobs presenting programmes on footballers' wives and trivial TV, had her heart set
on something more hard-hitting.

'I think I've got a lot to offer. I'd love to do a show like Oprah
Winfrey – there's not really an equivalent in the UK,' she told
The Sun. 'I could do it because I definitely have the passion.
I went on *This Week* with Diane Abbott and Michael Portillo. The
younger generation wouldn't normally tune in to something
like that but maybe they would if there were younger people on
the panel.

'And I was asked to go on a radio show the other day to talk
about politics. They even played my single. I didn't ask them to
– I just really wanted to get some stuff off my chest and have a
bit of a debate. I was buzzing afterwards!

'When I met the Prime Minister I told him I have always
wanted to get involved with politics. I said if he ever needed a
voice from the world of pop music to give me a call! I love news
and current affairs and want to use my fame in a positive way.
You can't change the world, but you can do your bit.'

And, in a week when Barack Obama finally made it to
the White House and Lewis Hamilton raced to victory in the
Formula One championship, she had plenty to get off her chest.
'History really has been made this week. They're mixed race but
the world views them as men of colour, so it's an amazing
achievement for both of them. I do feel in a way that it's strange
that it's 2008 and we are still seeing "firsts" – first black
American President, first black F1 champion. We obviously
still have a long way to go until skin colour just isn't an issue.
But the world is changing. Barack is so personable. I saw him
on Ellen DeGeneres' TV show, dancing to Beyoncé's 'Crazy In

Love'. He really connects with a younger audience and if that got people voting, that's brilliant.'

Political ambition aside, Alesha wasn't above a silly stunt to help sell the new album. She admitted she was embarrassed when a picture of her, dressed in a sumo suit at a Radio 1 event, made the papers. 'I had to dress up as a sumo wrestler and fight one of the presenters,' she laughed later. 'I thought it was for their website but a picture of me looking like a tosser in the costume ended up on the front of a local London paper!'

Even so, waiting to find out how her treasured new release would do in the album charts was a nail-biting time and she admitted she was worried about letting her record company down. 'The record label Atlantic have invested a lot of money which makes me nervous. It shows they believe in me, but God, I don't want to let them down. I am as excited as I am petrified. I think I have made the best album I could in the time I have had . . . I am not that confident at all. I can only do my best and hope it's good enough.'

The album debuted at number 26 in the album charts and peaked at number 11. A respectable return to form for the star, who soon had her mind on other things.

On 9 November, it was leaked on the BBC show *Something for the Weekend* that she would support Enrique Iglesias on his UK tour in the New Year. Even so, she had a bigger dream. 'Having my own world tour is my biggest dream,' she said. 'I'd love to have an amazing band and the big stage show people will come to see. I have wanted this since I was a little girl, so I am determined to do all I can to fulfill it.'

On the few occasions she wasn't working, Alesha was relaxing in the Hertfordshire home she shares with her cousin and her dog, a Collie cross called Roxy. 'My cousin lives with me so she looks after the dog and I pay my brother £25 a week to walk the dog after school,' she said on Radio 2. 'He loves walking her and whenever I can bring her somewhere I do. I haven't got one of those that sits on your handbag. There's no way he'd walk that!'

'I've had her three years,' she told Chris Moyles. 'I rescued her from the RSPCA. She's a troublesome dog. Only I would put up with her. She's got this growling temperament at night that scares my guests.'

A good homely girl, Alesha's idea of a perfect weekend's relaxation is a good roast dinner and a day spent catching up on her favourite programmes on Sky Plus, including, of course, *Strictly Come Dancing*. 'It's good to watch it,' she said of series six. 'I know what they're going through. I feel for them. I'm voting for a lot of them as well. I'd like Lisa Snowdon to win. She's a Welwyn Garden City girl, and a lovely girl, so I'm rooting for her.'

CHAPTER FIFTEEN

Breathe Slow

Christmas 2008 found Alesha once more wooing the nation with her beautiful ballroom for the *Strictly Come Dancing* Christmas Special. This time, the competition was even stiffer, with previous winners Jill Halfpenny and Tom Chambers as well as series six finalists Rachel Stevens and Lisa Snowdon taking part. Kelly Brook, who may well have challenged Alesha for the series five crown had she remained in the show, also returned to dance with Brian Fortuna as original partner Brendan Cole was once again paired with Lisa Snowdon.

Dancing with her close friend Matthew Cutler once more, Alesha looked a Christmas cracker in a stunning white ball gown with an enormous puffy skirt, and her Viennese waltz to the Otis Redding version of 'White Christmas' stunned the judges yet again. The first dance of the show, they gave it a fantastic score of 39 – still failing to clinch the elusive ten from Craig Revel Horwood – and looked like strong contenders for the title. However, as the evening progressed Kelly and Brian racked up 39 for their jive, Rachel and Vincent Simone scored the same for their rumba and so did Jill Halfpenny's American Smooth with Darren Bennett.

As had happened in the series before, a tie at the top of the table meant that those at the bottom could not be saved by the audience vote. In this case, the show was pre-recorded and the votes were coming from the studio audience, instead of the viewing public, but the show had to be stopped while Head Judge Len Goodman considered how to rank the top four couples.

'There was a four-way tie at the top of the leader board,' explained a BBC statement. 'In these circumstances Len Goodman ranks the tying couples. To allow for this contingency the show was stopped.'

After a nail-biting break for contestants and audience alike, Len delivered his verdict. Clearly impressed by the MC turned belle of the ball, he ranked Alesha top, followed by Jill, Rachel and then Kelly. After the audience vote, however, she and Matthew were left in third place behind winner Jill and runner-up Kelly.

In December, Alesha also won a peculiar accolade in that she was named the most sought-after celebrity of 2008. In a survey of 14,000 name searches on the internet, conducted by online media contacts directory Celebrities Worldwide, her name beat the likes of *Doctor Who* star David Tennant and controversial broadcaster Jonathan Ross.

'It's quite surprising that Alesha Dixon has been searched more times this year than stars like Lily Allen and Kylie Minogue,' said Celebrities Worldwide spokesman Richard Brecker. 'But Alesha's amazing in that she combines beauty and glamour while managing to come across as a down-to-earth girl who people seem to relate to and genuinely like. We think she must be a popular choice with many of the charities using our database and suspect she ticks all the right boxes – friendly, while being sexy, approachable and inoffensive at the same time. I guess the public have warmed to her as well since she ended her relationship with her husband, the former So Solid Crew star MC Harvey after his much publicized affair with singer Javine Hylton.'

Christmas 2008 also saw her performing at a concert to mark the turning on of the lights in Birmingham town centre, where she sang 'The Boy Does Nothing' and a solo version of 'Scandalous'.

And while the talks about her following fellow *Strictly* winner Jill Halfpenny into the West End show *Chicago* seemed to have come to nothing, she had her moment in the famous fishnets when she performed the most famous song from the show, 'All That Jazz', on the BBC1 New Year's Eve show, *The Big Finish*. Carried on stage by partner Matthew Cutler and Brendan Cole, Alesha was joined by the other *Strictly* dancers for a steamy routine that was sure to have the stage musical's producers begging for a second chance. It was a suitably glitzy end to another triumphant year for Alesha.

A short break over Christmas was followed by another holiday to see her dad in Thailand, but with Alesha's amazing energy levels, the return to work couldn't come too soon. 'I love working at the moment,' she said on her return. 'I've just had a ten-day holiday in Thailand and all I wanted was to get back to work. I'm in a good place right now.'

'Breathe Slow', her second single from *The Alesha Show*, was released in January and the singer was well aware of the importance of its success. 'The first single gets you up and off the block,' she said, 'but the second shows there's an album worth buying.'

An ode to keeping control in the face of emotional distress, the song advocates counting from one to ten and advises, 'Ladies never lose composure.' Perhaps another reference to the messy break-up with Harvey and the moments when she, understandably, felt she was losing control.

'The song was written for women about chilling and not losing your dignity,' explained Alesha. 'Losing your rag is not a class act.' And despite the line, 'I ain't the one to shoot the gun, because it means you'll be winning,' she didn't intend it to be a reference to gun crime, nor did she think it would make a difference if it was. 'Pop music is powerful but perhaps not that powerful!'

The video, shot in Las Vegas, seemed once again to hark back to Harvey, as the stunning singer is seen drinking coffee in a café in a raincoat before taking off a wedding ring and removing her coat to reveal a silver showgirl outfit. She then walks past the bright lights of the Strip, flirting with passers-by.

In fact, the video shoot brought Alesha more attention than she intended since it coincided with a well-publicized bout between UK boxer Ricky Hatton and American Paulie Malignaggi. Vegas was full of British boxing fans, and the main street came to a standstill as they all jostled to take a picture.

The beautiful ballad raced to number six in the UK charts on downloads alone and peaked at number three, one of her biggest hits to date. And the song also became the perfect soundtrack to her next big adventure, a charity climb to the peak of Kilimanjaro.

Six months earlier, Alesha had signed up to climb Africa's highest peak to raise money for Comic Relief, along with Take That's Gary Barlow, presenters Denise Van Outen, Fearne Cotton and Ben Shephard, Girls Aloud stars Kimberley Walsh and Cheryl Cole, Boyzone frontman Ronan Keating and DJ Chris Moyles.

As the challenge to reach the peak drew nearer, it became clear that Alesha wasn't necessarily in the peak of fitness. Four months on *Strictly* had built up her stamina, but in the intervening year she admitted she hadn't kept up the momentum. 'Everyone thinks I'm still dancing, but it's been more than twelve months since I was training for *Strictly*,' she told *The Sun*. 'I went on the treadmill the other day and when I came off my thighs were killing me. It's not a good look for girls to have big, muscly thighs, so I've got to be careful with the training. I've done a few walks though, which have been pretty hard. Three hours on the treadmill is tough going. I didn't say "Yes" to doing this straight away because I realized how tough the challenge was going to be. It is worth it, though. Comic Relief is a brilliant charity.'

Happy as ever with her own figure, she hit out, in another interview, at media images of skinny celebs and begged women to stop being so critical of themselves. 'Someone like Victoria Beckham is beautiful in her own right but women shouldn't want to look like her,' she told the *Mirror*. 'Why can't we just be happy with ourselves? You're never going to look your best if you're feeling rubbish about yourself. We're our own worst critics and we need to stop.'

She also had high praise for climbing buddy and Girls Aloud stunner Cheryl Cole. 'For me it's about what shines within,' she said. 'Some women are aesthetically beautiful but they're cold people. Cheryl Cole may be flawless but she also gives out a warm energy and without that she wouldn't be as beautiful – that's what draws people to her.'

And, while *Strictly* fans had got used to her being dolled up to the nines in shimmering ballgowns and sexy salsa dresses, the thirty-year-old singer claimed she felt better in trainers. 'I feel sexiest when I'm walking out of the gym after a workout. I feel like I glow even though I'm probably a bit sweaty.'

As the mountain loomed ahead, Alesha was excited about the adventure and couldn't wait to begin. And she was looking forward to spending time with controversial DJ Chris Moyles. After a guest spot on his Radio 1 show she blogged, 'Chris Moyles is great fun – he takes the mickey out of me, I take the mickey out of him: I just laughed the whole time. I even got him to play a snippet of an album track called "Let's Get Excited". I was a little nervous because you know what Chris is like – he could eat you alive if he wanted to! But I'm walking Mount Kilimanjaro with Chris in February 2009 so he couldn't have given me a hard time – I'd have made his life hell on the mountain.'

Kilimanjaro is an inactive stratovolcano which rises above the plains of Tanzania and is the highest peak in Africa at 5,895 metres (19,340 ft). A sign at the top of Uhuru peak, where the celebrities were heading, announces 'Congratulations. You are now at Uhuru Peak, Tanzania, Africa's Highest Mountain. The World's Highest freestanding mountain.' It's a difficult climb, and of the 20,000 people a year who attempt it, a third don't make it.

Team leader Gary Barlow was amazed that so many celebrities were up for the charity challenge. 'Everyone has been great,' he marvelled. 'I thought I would have to have a huge list of people and work my way down because they wouldn't want to do it. But more or less everyone I asked was up for it. It started off because I just wanted a challenge and to raise money for a great cause like Comic Relief.'

As well as training in the gym, the group attended a lecture at the National Olympic Centre, where they were tested for their ability to cope with the altitude by going through a work-out in a specially adapted chamber. Surprisingly, overweight DJ Chris Moyles came top of the table.

'Physically, it is going to be tough,' said Alesha. 'But the biggest struggle we are going to have is with ourselves. I think, mentally, we're all going to be put to the test.'

Alesha was so keen to start, she and *GMTV* presenter Ben Shephard flew out to Tanzania a few days early to get their bearings. In a video diary, when she first spotted the top of the mountain, she was astonished and not a little daunted by the task ahead. 'It's unbelievable, I have to say, because I was look-ing at it thinking, "Everyone said it was going to be such a steady climb and it's seriously steep." How are we going to do that?'

Ben explained that they would be 'traversing' the sides of the mountain in a zig-zag fashion.

'And what's the crack with the snow?' asked Alesha. 'We don't know that, do we? Because it's hot here and the higher up we get the more we're going to burn – but there's snow. There are people watching this that are thinking we are seriously thick! Looking at it, it's amazing to think we are going to do that. I seriously don't know how we're going to do that. But it's beautiful. To be that high up will be such a treat.'

The day before setting off on their epic eight-day journey, Alesha and the other climbers visited a local village where they were greeted with open arms. The singer talked to children affected by malaria in Ngare Naiyobi village.

'Across Africa malaria kills more children than any other disease, with 3,000 youngsters being taken by it every day,' said team mate Gary afterwards. 'One of the biggest reasons for this is people can't afford the simple nets that would offer them and their kids protection. The cost of supplying a net to a family and educating them on the importance of using it is just £5. All of us who are taking on this climb want to give as many families as possible the chance to protect themselves.'

Alesha also went on the rounds with the local district nurse, who deals with tragic malaria cases every day. In one village she met a malaria widow who had the disease herself, as did her six children. The experience was an eye opener for the Welwyn Garden City girl. 'In a family with no malaria nets the disease spreads fast,' said Alesha. 'I can't begin to imagine how this lady feels. They have no protection, none. And it's the repetition of having it, treating it, then it coming back again. It's a cycle, and at some point we need to put a clog in that cycle. People in Britain take things for granted. We complain about our NHS system and yes, it's not perfect, but it's far better than what they have here. We've got a cheek to complain, that's what I think. It's such a simple thing. We're not asking to change the world. It's just a net.

'Even walking the mountain we've got more luxuries than they've got here. I feel like if I moan on that mountain I have to slap myself around the face. How dare I!'

On 1 March 2009, the nine celebs took their first tentative steps on the steep side of the mountain. Surrounded by guides and porters, and weighed down with rucksacks, the brave group were led by singer-songwriter Gary Barlow, knowing that, before they had even set out, they had raised nearly £500,000 for Comic Relief.

Expedition guide Raj, an experienced climber, had a team with him to help the celebrities on their way, and Ronan, for one, was glad they were on hand. 'Raj and his team are brilliant,' he said. 'I wouldn't want to be going up the mountain without them. They really know what they're doing. Raj has been up Everest twice, which is very impressive.'

'My foot is swollen,' said Alesha as they arrived at Kilimanjaro National Park. 'Not the best way to start.' She wasn't the only one with problems.

'Both Cheryl and I have problems with our feet, which come from years of dancing in high heels,' revealed Kimberley Walsh. 'It has done something to the nerves, which makes our toes hurt.'

And Gary damaged his spine while training just days before flying out to Africa and the bumpy jeep ride to the park only made matters worse. 'After that horrendous car journey, I've completely seized up,' he worried. 'But I'm just thinking a day at a time, really. That's all I can do.'

Leaving base camp early in the morning, with Alesha clutching her trusty bag of Minstrels, the climbers trekked through the difficult terrain of the rainforest and had to stop after four hours because of the heat. But the enthusiasm among the team was amazing and spirits were high.

'We've just done a serious bit of climbing,' said Ben Shephard, indicating Alesha and Fearne over his shoulder. 'And Hinge and Bracket were chatting away like they were just going for a stroll in the park.' After disturbing an ant's nest, Alesha's stroll turned into a sprint as she cackled her famous laugh and joked, 'Have you ever seen anyone get up a mountain quicker!'

It didn't take long for reality to hit. As they bedded down in their tents on the second day, at 3,500 feet, most of them were already showing signs of altitude sickness.

Guide Raj revealed that many were suffering headaches and sickness and the high temperature experienced at the bottom of the mountain had been replaced by freezing conditions. 'We're on day two of Kilimanjaro,' he said in the documentary made for Comic Relief. 'We covered quite a climb today, about 700 metres. The crew did well today, a tough, seven-hour day. Now we're at camp they're starting to feel the altitude and some of them have symptoms of acute mountain sickness – headache and a bit of sickness. Nothing to worry about but we'll have to keep a close eye on them because this is where its starts getting more serious, we're now at 3,500 metres. The temperature drops and it can drop well below freezing.'

However, there were benefits too. The high altitude also made the group incredibly giggly, which they quite enjoyed, crying with laughter at the slightest gag.

That day also saw Alesha have a close call during a call of nature. Having walked away from the group to pee behind a bush, she lost her footing and fell a few feet down the mountain. She saved herself from falling further by grabbing onto some tree branches. 'For a split second we really thought we had lost her because she fell so far down,' said a team member. 'Needless to say she was very embarrassed to have slipped while having a wee.'

Day three was Ronan Keating's birthday and the other eight decorated the breakfast tent and sang Stevie Wonder's version of 'Happy Birthday', as he entered. 'It was very funny,' said Ronan. 'Everyone was trying to keep me out of the breakfast tent while we were all getting ready this morning. I walked into the breakfast tent and there it is all set up with a balloon and a lovely birthday card and they all sang "Happy Birthday". It was quite a special happy birthday with Girls Aloud, Gary Barlow, Alesha Dixon, all these big mega stars, and of course Ben Shephard, singing "Happy Birthday". It was brilliant. It was really, really great.'

Gary's back problem had worsened and he was forced to take a short cut with a couple of guides. 'Every step is agony,' he said. 'I'm disappointed that I've had to take a different route. This morning was the first time I thought I might not do it, might not get there. I'm gutted.'

Spirits were further dampened when the team's medics spotted a young British climber on the mountain who was suffering from severe altitude sickness and had to be stretchered down. Left any longer he may well have died. The whole group was shocked. 'To see someone stretchered down on oxygen really hit me,' said Ben Shephard. 'His eyes were rolling in his head,' gasped Ronan. 'It's a wake-up call,' admitted Alesha. 'It's the reality of where we really are.'

That reality was about to get even more stark. That night, Fearne had to be given an injection after collapsing outside the toilet tent. Gary Barlow recorded the incident in his climb diary. 'Bad night in the camp,' he wrote. 'Disaster struck in tent six. At midnight we were woken by Fearne calling out for help. She had got up to go to the loo and collapsed on the floor outside from exhaustion and was too weak to move. Fearne was given an anti-sickness injection but when we woke this morning she still didn't look good.'

By day four, Alesha was also feeling the effects of the lack of oxygen. After complaining she couldn't breathe, she said, 'I don't want to stop. I feel drunk – so that's not bad I suppose,' before collapsing in helpless giggles.

Despite suffering severe symptoms of altitude sickness, Fearne made it to camp that night, to be greeted with hugs and cheers from her fellow climbers. Now at 4,600 metres they were warned that the sickness could hit them harder in the next six or eight hours.

'Today's been really funny because when I woke up this morning I was breathing calmly, I didn't have a headache, I had a good breakfast,' Alesha revealed. 'And the minute I put my backpack on I just felt really emotional. For the first 200 metres of the walk I was just crying! I don't know why. Then I really started to enjoy it, relaxed, I could see the top of the mountain, it was beautiful. It was really enjoyable. Then, a little bit further on, I just felt really dizzy, so I've had to stop and I'm going to stay at the back because I don't want to slow anyone down. It feels like you're drunk, that's the only way I can describe it. I don't feel sick or anything like that – I feel like I just need to go at a Jamaican pace. When I was dizzy, and I had to be escorted over to a rock, I felt like a wally, because you don't want to be a drama queen. I stood behind this rock and said, "Please, God, get me to the top of this mountain." You actually feel like you have to pray. It's more of a mental battle than it is physical because my legs and feet feel fine. It's weird, but walking is the easiest part. It's all in the mind.'

And Alesha admitted she had worked out a mental strategy to get her to the summit. 'I'm going to keep going and take my time and focus on the next camp, rather than the top, although that's difficult when you can actually see it.'

Kimberley explained that the girls were keeping each other strong. 'We're staying upbeat and, as a group, somehow getting ourselves through it. In the morning you wake up and its still dark, there's frost on the tent and you have to get up and go to the toilet with your knees knocking together, but me, Cheryl and Alesha share a tent, so we wake up in the morning, look at each other and think, "Is this really happening?" and try and help each other through it.'

Alesha admitted Fearne's bravery on the mountain had spurred her on. 'At one point I was sitting down, a loner on a rock, and I saw Fearne coming in the distance and I thought, "If she's doing it, that's it. I'm getting up, because she's suffered far worse than anyone."

The next to fall victim was *X Factor* judge Cheryl Cole, who was also given a jab to help her carry on after being sick at breakfast time. 'I crawled out of my tent and got a whiff of the food, and then it was projectile vomit,' she told the camera. 'It was coming out of my mouth, out of my nose . . . The doctor gave me an injection which is killing my bottom for the eight-hour walk, but I feel like a new woman!'

Despite their suffering, on day five the whole team made it up the Barranco Wall, a terrifying 250-foot climb up a sheer rockface. Chris Moyles once more conquered his fear of heights and told Radio 1 later that day. 'I still think not many people know how tough this is. It's way, way, way harder than I thought it would be. We had to climb this part of the mountain today literally on our hands and knees and I'm scared of heights. Luckily it was so cloudy that I couldn't see how high we were!'

The intrepid climbers were rewarded by a severe drenching, as the heavens opened for the first time since they embarked on their adventure. But there was good news when they reached camp and discovered that they had already reached their fundraising target of £1 million.

On day six, it was time to head for high camp, just below the summit of the mountain. While Cheryl was forcing herself 'to walk like a snail,' Alesha was raring to go. 'My theory is to get to the top as quickly as we can and be out of breath when we get there.'

Fearne was feeling fitter and determined to make it. 'She's the superstar of the climb,' said Ronan. 'We can't believe she's still going.'

'The magical feeling of normality is not to be underestimated,' Fearne joked. 'Don't take it for granted.'

At dinner that night, just before the team took their final steps to the peak, Raj warned them 'this could be the hardest thing you've done, mentally and physically, in your lives.' As the daytime temperatures make climbing to the summit more dangerous, climbers have to set out at night, in the dark, braving sub-zero conditions. The nine celebrities and their party set out at 12.20am in a seventy-five-miles-per-hour wind and a temperature of minus twenty degrees celcius. The oxygen level in the air was at 50 per cent and the group had to wear hats with torches to see where they were going.

Just after 6.30am, as the sun came up over the horizon, the first of the party reached the peak. Emotions ran high, with Denise and Cheryl in tears, Fearne saying, 'I can't believe I've done it!' According to the Comic Relief blog, Ben, Fearne, Denise and Cheryl make it first, followed by Kimberley Walsh, Ronan Keating and Gary Barlow, all three of whom were said to be 'in agony'.

'Seemed like a hair-brained plan six months ago but somehow we're here,' marvelled Gary. 'I can't believe it! Stretcher for Barlow!'

Chris Moyles came next, hugging the wooden sign that marks the highest point in Africa, and Alesha was the last one up to the top, arriving at 7.55am and immediately lying on the floor, saying, 'Night,' and laughing her infectious giggle. She had, the blog reported, 'been through the pain barrier', to finish at the top. She was said to have been in severe pain but had refused to stop.

The titanic effort of these celebrities, who by their own admission were used to jumping in cabs to 'get from Notting Hill to Kensington', had raised £1.5 million for Comic Relief – rising eventually to £3 million – which made every minute of agony worthwhile.

'The challenge was totally underestimated by every one of us,' admitted Gary. 'The climb was the hardest thing I've ever done. I never want to see a tent or a sleeping bag again! To be told each day the amount we had raised kept our spirits up. So thank you so much to the beautiful British public for being so generous.'

Yet again, the comeback queen had set herself a gruelling challenge and, through determination and sheer guts, had carried it through to the end.

Alesha was once more on top of the world.

CHAPTER SIXTEEN

Back on Solid Ground

On her return to the UK Alesha was tired but understandably delighted that she had fulfilled her promise to make it to the top of Africa's highest peak. On hearing the news that the donations had peaked at £3 million she revealed that the thought of those she had met in Africa had spurred her on through the tough ordeal.

'To me it's so important that we raised that much money because I feel like, for the public to give money they have to see you do something extreme that warrants and deserves them picking up the phone,' she told the *Birmingham Mail*. 'For me, I wanted to get out to Africa and spend some time with the people there, finding out why I was doing the climb, where the money would be going and how it would be helping people. That helped me a lot because when I was climbing the mountain I thought about it a lot, the cause and the money being raised.'

She admitted that, before she got the call from Gary Barlow, she would never have considered putting herself through such a traumatic trial. 'To be honest with you it's not something I would have done for fun! I really did struggle and I found it a really tough thing Everybody that did it thought, "This is a once-in-a-lifetime thing to do," and it really was life-changing, but at the time it was hard. We had great fun as a group together. We all got on extremely well but the thing that got us to the top of the mountain was knowing that people were ringing up donating.'

However, being exhausted from the climb, it wasn't for a few days that Alesha could truly take stock of her amazing achievement. 'I came back from it feeling a bit drained and spaced out,' she recalled in an interview with the *Birmingham Mail*. 'It didn't quite sink in. Everybody was saying, "Well done. You should be proud." And I couldn't quite take that in at the time. On reflection, I'm glad I did it, I definitely learnt a lot while I was doing it, and there comes a point in your life when some things are more important than what you are doing. There have to be moments in life when it's not about you; selfless moments.

'The crisis in Africa is so serious and we are so fortunate in this country, we're so lucky and it's really important that we all do our bit for others. I did hesitate because I never do things half-heartedly and I don't make rash decisions but you go there and spend time with the people and you feel like you can't do enough to help.

'In my little world there's so much I want to do, but life is about the journey along the way, and it's about the experience of a lot of things as opposed to the end result. For me it's about finding what will make me grow and experiencing different things – that's what life's all about.'

In another interview she admitted that her usual upbeat persona was dragged down by the rare climate and tough climb. 'It was really tough, probably the hardest thing I have done in my life, and I came back from there scared and tired,' she told the *South Wales Echo*. 'I'm trying to be careful here because I don't want to be negative about it. Lots of good came out of it – we raised £3m for charity – but for me it was a struggle. The altitude affects your emotions, and as the oxygen levels got thinner, it affected my spirits. And just walking for eight hours at a time, it's hard to stay focussed, so the only way I could maintain focus was thinking about the people we were doing it for.'

No sooner had she climbed down from the mountain than she was setting herself another challenge – this time to break a record. On 2 April 2009, Alesha gathered a huge audience in Buckinghamshire to attempt to smash the record for the most choreographed backing dancers. The stunt, for Sky 1's *Guinness World Records Smashed*, took place in front of an audience and competition winners and saw Alesha perform her soon to be released single, 'Let's Get Excited', surrounded by no less than 329 dancers. Needless to say she broke the record!

The single, due for release on 11 May, was a frenetic dance track where Alesha urged her fans to, 'Do it the Madonna way', and 'Get into the groove'. Co-written and produced by Redzone, who were behind a string of hits, including 'Single Ladies', by Alesha's heroine Beyoncé, and Rihanna's unforgettable 'Umbrella', it was written and recorded during just two sessions in London and LA.

The video started with a quintessential Alesha look – a very short skirt and shiny straightened hair, which she strokes lovingly – but she soon changed into a Madonna-style outfit of leather trousers, bondage-style black basque and hair pulled tightly back from her face into one flowing ponytail. Like the record-breaking performance, it sees her performing a speedy routine in front of a large room full of dancers, choreographed by Tone Talauega, who had been responsible for the iconic silhouette iPod commercials, Madonna and Justin Timberlake's '4 Minutes' video and Pink's latest tour.

Promoting the single on Justin Lee Collins' Channel Four chat show, Alesha shocked her host by receiving a marriage proposal from an audience member as soon as she sat down. With her short-lived marriage now way behind her, the divorced diva could finally start to laugh at the situation.

'Been there, got the T-shirt!' she fired back to a roar of laughter from the crowd, then she revealed, 'I was proposed to by a female at the weekend. I was really happy. The first time I have been chatted up by a woman. I really liked that. She said she was going to grab my bum, though! She said, "I was tempted to grab your bum but I thought it might be a bit inappropriate."' Asked how she would have reacted to that, she replied, 'I have a tendency to do that, so I probably would have liked it. I like slapping people's bums.' Proposals aside, the singer was still single but was adamant that she wasn't looking too hard for a man. 'I've got to a point in my life where I accept it for what it is,' she told *OK!* magazine. 'I have friends who moan about not having a boyfriend and I want to tell them to get a grip – desperation won't attract someone into your life! I am open to meeting somebody, and I do believe there is someone out there who's right for me, but I'm also happy just doing my thing. I'm thirty now but I'd love to think that in the second half of my thirties I could become a mum. I tried planning things once in my life and they didn't go to plan, so my new motto in life is to just focus on the day and the weeks ahead and let the future take care of itself. Whatever the end result is, then that's my destiny, whether there's a family in there or not, it's beyond my control.'

In an interview with the *Daily Mail* she admitted that the barriers had gone up after her split from Harvey and that she had actively discouraged new relationships.

'I did put a fence around myself as a protection and I made a conscious decision not to have a boyfriend because part of me was aware that I was still dealing with the last relationship,' she said. 'I was healing from that in order to be in a healthy place again where I could be open to another – and I am open now to meeting somebody new.'

On *The Chris Moyles Show*, before the pair set foot on Kilimanjaro, the cheeky DJ had asked Alesha why she was single and added, 'Are you high maintenance?'

'I don't think I am. I'm a very self-sufficient lady. I don't have a social life, really. I'm married to my work right now.'

Asked what sort of man she would go for she replied, 'Men with a good sense of humour. Being good at cooking would be a plus. An animal lover.'

In the midst of the 'Let's Get Excited' promotion, the busy beauty had something to really get excited about. On 7 May she began her tour with Latin heartthrob Enrique Iglesias, who had personally picked her after seeing her perform on a TV show. 'I've had more of my male friends asking about him than female friends,' she laughed.

Sadly the gorgeous Spaniard was taken, by stunning tennis ace Anna Kournikova, but Alesha had plenty more men knocking on her dressing room door, including R&B flavour of the month Ne-Yo. 'I was shocked,' said an impressed Alesha. 'He's so nice; he said he loved my "wash-up, brush-up" song.'

One guy it seemed she wasn't getting on so well with was Enrique himself – or at least his entourage. Having banned her from using the crooner's personal stage catwalk, they upset Alesha further by accusing her of emptying effluent outside one of the buildings they stopped at. 'They summoned my manager down and said, "Have you just emptied the chemical toilet outside the production centre?"' she told Key 103 radio station, Manchester. 'It was soapy water. We're not hillbillies!'

Alesha's ass-kicking turn at the top of the show went down a storm with audiences and critics alike. 'It's not often a support act outshines the headliner,' wrote Gordon Barr of Newcastle's *Evening Chronicle*. 'But Alesha Dixon did just that as she performed to a near-capacity crowd at the Arena last night. After our Cheryl, Alesha is perhaps the closest thing to a national pop treasure we have at the moment, and she showed us why last night. There was no fancy set design, no pyrotechnics, just Alesha, her music – and a couple of lads helping with the dance routines, although, as we know, she doesn't need much help, being a former *Strictly* champ herself. It was all we needed, as her voice and personality shone through as she performed her all-too-brief set.'

Despite the training and mountain climb that had seen her at the peak of fitness two months before, she admitted the live performances were hard. And despite shunning the after-party lifestyle to be in bed by 10pm because she didn't want to 'let the crowd down', she admitted to feeling her age.

'I look back at the time when I was in Mis-Teeq and wonder how I did it,' she said. 'I remember doing shows and feeling like I could carry on afterwards – you definitely feel it when you turn thirty, trust me.'

Even so, she was happily using the two-week stint as a welcome warm-up to the main event – her own headline tour. In the midst of the Enrique tour she announced that she would embark on seventeen dates around the country in October. *The Alesha Show*, as the tour was, unsurprisingly, called, promised to be the ultimate in pop entertainment after Tone Talauega once more got involved in the choreography. 'I'm pulling in the choreographer who did the last Madonna tour and Michael Jackson for eleven years,' said Alesha. But given how tough she had found the Enrique tour, she was being sensible about the amount of dancing involved and made sure there were a few ballads dotted throughout the set, which allowed her to, erm, 'Breathe Slow'.

'I have to say, when I came up with the idea of doing this dance breakdown that we're doing I thought, "What am I doing?" One of the dancers hands me the microphone and I'm just gasping for breath. There are some frantic moments, but there is a section when the boys go away and it's just me singing three or four down-tempo records. I get my breath back, and it's a really nice moment where I can show a different side to me. The beginning of the show is fun, then there's a middle that's more intimate, and then we pick up the pace again. Hopefully we'll all be very fit.'

To inject a little humour into the proceedings, she promised a reworking of the classic Cameron Diaz dance from the Jim Carrey comedy *The Mask*. The nightclub dance in the 1994 movie made the actress into a huge star and Alesha planned her own version for the tour. 'The whole point of the album being called *The Alesha Show* is that it is just that – a show we can take in any direction we want,' she told *The Mail on Sunday*. 'We're doing a big dance breakdown to *The Mask*'s 'Hey, Pachuco' – the music from that Cameron Diaz scene everyone remembers.

It's got a real big-band feel, with samba and Charleston moves. We did some shows last weekend and launched into this dancing which blew the audience away . . . We'll expand it even more for October.'

With a set based on the fast-selling album, Alesha looked forward to providing an entertaining night out. 'Obviously it's going to be showcasing *The Alesha Show* album. It's going to be lots of fun. The great thing about the tour is that it's for people that have bought the album and enjoyed it, it's a way to come out and celebrate that. I can give something back to them.'

And with her new army of *Strictly* fans likely to be clamouring for tickets to the concerts, she vowed to put some Latin and ballroom into the choreography. 'There has definitely been a big influence from *Strictly* on the tour. I learned all those amazing dances and now this is my chance to use them.'

As usual life was moving at a frantic pace. She had sold 750,000 records over the last six months and was finally enjoying international success, with 'The Boy Does Nothing' sitting in Europe's Top 10 airplay for four months and reaching number 2 in the French charts. She was keen to capitalize on her popularity on the continent before trying, once more, to crack America.

'I definitely want to go to America at some point,' she said. 'At the moment I'm concentrating on Europe. I'm having so much fun travelling to the different territories. I'm thinking of going to the studio and getting some more tracks done this year, and I've still got my tour coming up in October, so I don't know when I would have the chance to go to America, but it definitely would be on the agenda. Maybe in 2010.'

As well as the two tours, the single's promotion and the constant filming of the documentary *Being Alesha*, she was clearly thinking about the next album already. And she was planning a collaboration with fellow mountain climber Gary Barlow. 'I would love to do a collaboration,' she confirmed. 'Gary is an extraordinary songwriter and a great guy – it would be an honour to work with him.'

She also fancied getting together with tent buddy Cheryl Cole, as well other UK artists, to form the ultimate girl band. 'There are so many great British women at the moment and I'd love to set up a collaboration between them. They do super groups in America all the time but it would be great to get the girls together to do our own Brit version.

'I absolutely love Lily Allen's new stuff and Cheryl and I have talked about doing something before. It would make a brilliant charity record.'

At the same time the Topshop and Morgan fan found herself being fêted by two of the biggest names in designer fashion, Dolce & Gabbana. The Italian twosome were bowled over by her look in the video for 'The Boy Does Nothing' and started bombarding her with high-end gifts.

'Domenico and Stefano got in touch via my Italian label after seeing me on MTV and said they wanted to take me under their wing,' she laughed. 'I was like, great! I'll fly under your wing any day!'

Alesha's feet had hardly touched the ground since her first twirl on *Strictly Come Dancing*, but in the whirlwind of success, her head stayed firmly on her shoulders. 'I remember speaking to Lionel Richie at the BRITs last year and he gave me some advice,' she revealed, in the *South Wales Echo*. 'He said, "If you are at home for more than four days in this business then something's wrong." In this industry, there are no guarantees that your career is going to last, so you have to maximize your career at all times, particularly when you are younger and have the energy. I want to work hard now because I don't want to look back in years to come and think I could have done more.'

With a film role in *Milestones,* starring Brian Cox and Andy Garcia, still in the pipeline, Alesha was conquering the entertainment world genre by genre. 'You might as well aim as high as you possibly can, and if something happens along the way and you don't quite make it, then fair enough, but you might as well start off believing that it's possible,' was her philosophy. 'The great thing about *Milestones* is there's a song in the film that I was able to write and I'm playing a character that reflects part of my life. The story is about musicians who have come from a rough background. It's not a rags-to-riches story so much as an inspirational story.'

Despite her incredible schedule, the opinionated star still found time to blast the celebrity culture and berate society for its warped view of women.

Now Alesha, thirty, has had her say. 'The younger generation can only be influenced by what they are fed, so they look up to her,' she told Smooth Radio. 'It would be better if people like Marie Curie or someone who made a difference to the world were celebrated in the media.'

And she waded into the row over *Britain's Got Talent* singer Susan Boyle, who despite her dowdy appearance had wowed the crowd and the judges with her amazing operatic tones. Asked by the *Western Mail* if the middle-aged reality-show star was right to get a makeover in the wake of her first appearance on the show, Alesha replied, 'It's her body and her skin. It's about expressing who you are, not what you look like. The Susan

Boyle thing is just a perfect illustration of the fact that we should never judge a book by its cover, because a lot of people thought she was going to be a joke, purely because of the way she looked, yet she had a beautiful voice. I think in this country we are guilty of putting people on a pedestal for looking a certain way but, thankfully, in this country it is also about character – and she proved she has character.'

Alongside her other projects, brand Alesha was going strong. She'd fronted the safe-sex campaign and now she got to endorse the two other things closest to a girl's heart – chocolate and fashion.

In May she joined forces with shoe store Dune to launch a fabulous necklace for charity. Profits from the £20 gold, silver and pewter coloured beads were to be donated to the Teenage Cancer Trust and Alesha stated, 'I can remember how hard it was being a teenager, but to have to deal with cancer too must completely turn your world upside down.'

In June, she teamed up with online retailers ASOS.com to offer fashion tips to customers, and also fronted a Toblerone campaign, offering chocolate-lovers a free download of her track 'Before The Sun Goes Down'. Fans could also win free tickets to her forthcoming tour and a chance to meet their idol in person. 'We're delighted to have Alesha on board – she's a great personality and the perfect fit with the brand,' said the firm's marketing manager. 'As a fun, quality brand, Toblerone is a great fit with Alesha's winning personality and upbeat pop sound,' said a spokesman at her label.

The same month she became an official ambassador for the charity Help a London Child, for whom she had completed a 10K run the previous summer. In a statement, she said, 'I am very honoured that Help a London Child have asked me to be an ambassador and I have accepted. I have supported the charity for some time now and it makes sense to make my involvement more official. I am looking forward to continuing my support and I have already volunteered to run the Royal Parks Foundation Half Marathon to help raise funds for the charity!'

'Alesha's thoughtfulness and compassion make her the perfect ambassador and we look forward to her continued invaluable support,' added the charity's spokeswoman, Kate Crabtree.

Finally, as Wimbledon approached, Alesha got together with sponsors Robinsons to encourage youngsters to take up tennis. As well as getting to attend the highlight of the tennis calendar, she landed herself some free coaching from the UK's former number one, Tim Henman.

On the opening day of the tournament, in June 2009, Alesha and Tim were on hand to play enthusiasts waiting in the queue to get in. 'I was asked by Robinsons if I wanted to have some training with Tim Henman, and I couldn't resist that,' she explained. 'He's great. I've always been a massive, massive fan of tennis. I love a challenge and I like keeping fit. I thought it was a good way of learning a new skill or getting fit for my live shows. And Tim is so lovely. He's been really sweet, and he says I'm really good, so result!'

And she revealed that she had been eating more healthily to try and get into shape. 'I eat what I want, when I want, but I try to eat healthy,' she said. 'Today, because I'd come to play tennis, I had fruit for breakfast and yoghurt. I don't deprive myself of anything. I just believe in everything in moderation, really.'

Talking at the event, Alesha revealed that she had been in talks about bringing *The Alesha Show* to life on television, but admitted that finding time to fit it in was proving a problem. And she also spilled the beans on another issue-driven documentary soon to be aired.

'It's about absent fathers. It's quite hard-hitting. The last documentary I did with them was called *Look but Don't Touch*, which focused on the digital age. The absent fathers documentary will be an eye-opener, and a lot of people will find it very, very helpful and very interesting. I'm thinking about doing a documentary on mixed race as well, which is in light of Obama and because the world is changing and constantly evolving. It will be great to have a documentary that documents race through the years.'

Preparing for her forthcoming tour, one of Alesha's favourite subjects – food – was on her mind. 'It's important to be open to new foods,' she asserted. 'I have a rule when I'm touring with the band that we all have to try a local dish in each country we visit. I love trying fish and seafood, and sushi is a big favourite of mine.'

Her diverse background means she will try anything that comes on a plate and, with the opportunities to travel that the recent years had afforded her, she has had plenty of time to sample local wares.

'The company that you keep is the most important thing,' she told *The Telegraph*. 'And the food. If I go somewhere and the food is not good that would ruin the whole holiday. Going out to eat is one of the most enjoyable things about going away, and I do like to try the local delicacies. I'm very open-minded with food, and I think when you go abroad that's the time to experiment and try something new.'

The summer saw her performing at the Isle of Wight and V Festivals as well as the trendy Summer Ball, where she found herself on the bill with old pals Blue. 'It reminded me of the days when I was in Mis-Teeq and we were all out on the road together and Blue was always one of my favourite bands because they were so down to earth, just really cool easy-going guys,' she said after the event.

Singer Duncan James was happy to return the compliment, saying, 'You know what? Alesha is wicked. I have just got to big her up because she has done so well and it's so nice to see like a British artist like Alesha. She's come from another band and she's just still there working and she's doing great, we love her.'

Every one, it seemed, loved Alesha. But her next move was about to plunge her into controversy – and even upset some of the *Strictly Come Dancing* fans who had been loyal in their support since her spectacular win.

CHAPTER SEVENTEEN

In the Eye of the Storm

As a contestant on *Strictly Come Dancing*, Alesha had confessed to being bit afraid of Arlene Phillips, and had revealed that the choreographer turned TV judge had upset her nan.

'Of all the judges, the one I'm most scared of is Arlene,' she admitted in *The Guardian* while taking part in the show. 'I adore her, though. She wants me to improve. The criticism is never negative. And anyway, I never take it personally, that would be just a little bit ungrateful.'

While supportive, Arlene had demanded nothing short of perfection and the singer commented, 'My nan was really cross about that. The thing is I'm *not* a professional dancer and I will never achieve absolute perfection. Though obviously it's flattering the judges have so much confidence in me – it makes me work harder.'

In the summer of 2009, Alesha found herself coming head to head with the fiery female judge, through no fault of her own.

The rumour mill began to churn out stories of Arlene Phillips' departure from *Strictly Come Dancing* in early June, and the truth was soon confirmed by sources at the BBC. The judge had been removed from the panel and had, instead, been given a slot talking about the series on *The One Show*.

The media were soon mentioning Alesha's name as a possible replacement, even as the producers were negotiating behind the scenes, and she seemed keen to join. 'I think once you are a part of *Strictly Come Dancing* you are part of the family and I do feel like that with the show,' she said. 'I have a love for it. It has helped carve out the next chapter of my career.'

In July, the BBC officially announced the inclusion of Alesha on the judges' panel, alongside male judges Len Goodman, Craig Revel Horwood and Bruno Tonioli. Prima ballerina Darcey Bussell would also be making an appearance as a guest judge towards the end of the series.

'As a former *Strictly* champion, Alesha knows exactly what it takes to win,' explained BBC1 Controller Jay Hunt. 'Her eye for great performance and her charisma and charm make Alesha a great addition to the judging panel.

'Darcey has impeccable credentials as a dancer and, as a guest judge, she will bring an exciting new dimension to the last few weeks of the *Strictly* competition.'

Alesha was thrilled to be back in the fold and said, 'I'm honoured and excited to be joining the judging panel. I've always felt like part of the *Strictly* family and really believe in the show.'

But this time Alesha had danced up a storm. The decision to replace the highly experienced choreographer with forty years in the business with a younger, less experienced series winner, caused an instant backlash, with the BBC being accused of being ageist and sexist. Even her new colleagues were unhappy with the decision.

Head judge Len Goodman, himself a sixty-five-year-old dance teacher and former Ballroom champ, accused the BBC of trying to sex up the programme saying, 'It sort of changes the whole dynamic of the panel maybe, which is a little bit scary. I hope the BBC are not trying to introduce a younger audience.

I would imagine the show attracts an older audience to what you get on *The X Factor*. I hope it does not affect the fan base.'

In another interview Len revealed that, despite their on-screen banter, he had a great deal of affection for the former judge. 'I will miss Arlene this year. I always got on very well with her and I have a great respect for her as a choreographer – she's probably the leading choreographer in the UK, if not the world . . . I do feel sorry for her, because we are friends.'

Australian choreographer Craig Revel Horwood admitted the three remaining judges were surprised by the BBC's decision to axe Arlene. 'I was shocked – very shocked – because I didn't think they would change it. I never thought they would change Arlene. I never thought they would change any of us,' he told *New!* magazine. 'It's going to be completely different without Arlene. I'm certainly going to miss her because I've literally grown up with her on the show. It is rather odd having someone new. But I suppose that's the way it is.'

And he cast doubts on the ability of the series five winner to fill Arlene's experienced shoes. 'She knows quite a bit about dance because she's been through the series and won it, so she's been trained by professionals and the best. But a celebrity contestant can never match someone who has been dancing their entire life, who has been competitive and in professional competitions.

'It's going to be different because Arlene and I argued a lot and had a lot of banter, and I don't know if Alesha and I will do that. I don't have a clue what will come out of her mouth, actually. The proof will be in the pudding.'

As complaints flooded into the BBC, celebrities, former contestants and even politicians had their say on the matter.

EastEnders star Louisa Lytton, who had appeared on the show in 2006 and also joined the judges on the live UK tour, was appalled. 'I was on the show a few years back now, but Arlene really looked after me. Her criticism was constructive, she taught me an awful lot and she cared about me on that show. It will be a great loss. It is a shame because she knows her stuff and that is what *Strictly Come Dancing* is about.'

Former contestant Esther Rantzen, writing in *The Daily Telegraph*, accused the BBC of underestimating the intelligence of its audience. 'We viewers recognize expertise and authority when we see it. There are plenty of us older women in the audience, and we want to see ourselves represented on mainstream, prime-time television. It's an insult to us, the viewers, to assume that we only watch women for their looks.'

She went on to say, 'We the viewers have had enough; we will no longer tolerate prejudice against age, particularly against ageing women. We, the ageing majority, demand and deserve respect for older people, including those on our screens.'

She did have some words of encouragement for Alesha, however, writing, 'So now the charming, but inexperienced, Alesha Dixon has been appointed on to *Strictly*'s judging panel. Let's not criticize her before she begins. She will bring first-hand knowledge of (in my own experience) the most terrifying competition on television. She knows what it feels like to stand at the back of the set, listening to the title music, and realize that there is no way back. And unlike me, she knows just how much hard work it takes to go from being a total novice to becoming a ballroom champion. Given the chance, Alesha may reveal a charming personality and a lively brain, so that she can make a real contribution to the show.'

Amazingly, the row even reached parliament, with government minister Harriet Harman stepping in to condemn the BBC over its attitude to older women. 'I think it's absolutely shocking that Arlene Phillips is not going to be a judge on *Strictly Come Dancing*,' she told the House of Commons. 'And as Equality Minister, I am suspicious that there is age discrimination there. So I'd like to take the opportunity of telling the BBC – it is not too late, we want Arlene Phillips in the next edition of *Strictly*.'

After more than 1,400 complaints flooded in, the BBC defended its decision and claimed there was no sexism involved. 'Age or gender has absolutely nothing to do with the decision to replace Arlene on the judging panel,' a spokeswoman claimed. 'The BBC has numerous mature presenters, including females, in prime-time shows. *Strictly* appeals to a wide audience and the BBC has been striving to ensure it stays fresh and relevant for existing viewers and newcomers. Every year the producers consider everything from the celebrities, guest performances, to the dancers and the overall look and feel. So the decision to replace Arlene and not one of the other judges was taken as a result of the review process, with the balance and flavour of the panel in mind and nothing else.'

On the corporation's complaints website, the following statement was published: 'We wanted to review *Strictly Come Dancing*'s format this year as we felt it was the right time to do so. Part of that process was reviewing the judging panel. We decided it would be a good idea to bring in someone like Alesha Dixon, who adds a new voice to the judging panel and has an insight into what the dancers have to go through. We are very grateful for Arlene's six years on the show and are delighted she will be remaining close to the *Strictly* family with her new role as *The One Show*'s resident *Strictly* expert.'

Controller Jay Hunt claimed Arlene was the obvious choice to go during the review process. 'It was not an easy decision to take,' she explained. 'When I looked at the four people we had, Bruno is the joker, Craig is the Simon Cowell of the show and Len is the head judge. Arlene has elements of all of them, but when you look at it, Arlene was the obvious one to change.'

While Arlene herself kept a dignified silence throughout the whole row, Jay Hunt said that Arlene was 'disappointed' but also 'incredibly excited' about her new job on *The One Show*.

In her first TV interview since the shock news Arlene was asked how she felt about leaving the show, and the usually forthright lady refused to criticize her replacement. 'Look, you know – it's hard,' she said. 'Alesha's lovely and she's a lovely dancer. What more can I say? I can't say any more. I'm passionate about dance and I was passionate about the show.'

She admitted, however, that she would miss the show because 'it has been a big part of my life for six years'.

Alesha was also keeping a low profile, refusing to talk to the media about her new job and keeping out of the gossip columns as she prepared for both the show and the still-scheduled tour. But because of her new BBC role, she was also forced to disappoint her music fans by postponing three of her seventeen proposed dates.

On her official website the singer broke her silence on *Strictly* to apologize to her fans in Lincoln, Southampton and Brighton, who would be missing out on the autumn tour. 'I'm so sorry to all my fans for having to change some of my dates,' she said. 'I'm really looking forward to playing live. I can't wait for the tour to start as I have been working so hard for a long time to achieve my dream of my first solo tour. 'I hope everyone can understand due to the emotional connection I have with the show, it was an exciting opportunity I could not turn down.'

A MOBO Award nomination for Best UK Act added an extra boost to her perfect summer and, in August, there was a new love in her life – adopted puppy Daisy.

A long time supporter of The Pedigree Adoption Drive, she found her friend for Roxy, who she had adopted in October 2006, at a local rescue centre. 'The Pedigree Adoption Drive is a wonderful campaign, set up to help re-home abandoned and stray dogs,' she said on the charity's website, before the new adoption. 'My collie cross Roxy was one of these lost dogs and through campaigns such as this, I was able to bring her into my home and after a while her confidence came back, transforming her from a shy and gloomy pup into a happy adventurous dog. Please give to The Pedigree Adoption Drive to help give other dogs the same chance in life.'

Animal lover Alesha found crossbreed puppy Daisy at the RSPCA Southridge Animal Centre in South Mimms, and said, 'I took a drive up to RSPCA Southridge in July as I was on the lookout for a companion for my dog Roxy. I saw little eleven-week-old Daisy and fell in love with her straight away. Daisy has settled in with Roxy very well and they play together a lot. At the moment she is in the process of being house trained and is responding really well. She is a little darling.'

The centre's staff were equally delighted with their celebrity patron. 'Alesha is a lovely girl, very polite and unassuming,' said one. 'She absolutely loves animals and we were more than happy to place the second dog with her after she first adopted from us.'

In September, the new *Strictly* celebs were announced, with boxer Joe Calzaghe, actresses Lynda Bellingham, Zoe Lucker and Laila Rouass and rock wife Jo Wood among the contestants.

But the row rumbled on with *The One Show*'s presenter Adrian Chiles calling Arlene's axing 'absolute bloody nonsense' and Alesha's fellow Welwyn City Garden girl Lisa Snowdon, a former finalist, saying she enjoyed Arlene's bickering with Len Goodman. 'I'm interested to see how it changes the dynamic of the panel,' she said, 'I loved Len rolling his eyes at Arlene in his grouchy way. I'll miss that.'

But Alesha's co-contestant on series five, Kelly Brook, stepped in to defend her and insisted Arlene would bring so much to the show. 'It must be so hard for Alesha but she'll be fine. She's such an amazing dancer,' Kelly said. 'She looks amazing and has a great personality.'

Breaking her silence, finally, Alesha gave one syndicated interview where she avoided talking about the controversy and said she couldn't wait to take up her position on the judging panel. 'I am so excited about being a judge on *Strictly*,' she said. 'I absolutely loved competing on the programme and so now to be a judge is just so fantastic. The best thing about being a judge is the fact I will have the best seat in the house.

'I didn't have to think twice when I was asked. I love a new challenge. I'd like to think I will be a very honest judge. If I like something, then the celebrities will know about it. If I don't I will try to be constructive.'

She claimed her gruelling experiences on the show would make her a sympathetic judge. 'I have got great empathy with the celebrities taking part. I know exactly how they are feeling and all the different emotions they will go through at every stage of the *Strictly* competition.'

And, despite the reservations of her new colleagues, she was looking forward to working alongside the remaining three. 'I really liked all the other judges when I competed and I can't wait to work alongside them on the new series. I am sure there will be plenty of banter between us all because it is impossible for four people to agree – but *Strictly* is an entertainment show and the banter is part of the fun. I am very open-minded to people's opinions.

'I hope the celebrities taking part will go on the show with a drive to enjoy learning to dance and go into it with passion. Strictly is a once-in-a-lifetime experience and it is so much fun.'

The storm may have been raging around her but Alesha was facing one of the biggest opportunities of her career – and she was ready to rumba.

CHAPTER EIGHTEEN

The Show Must Go On...

'My thirties is the beginning of a new chapter,' said Alesha in 2009. 'I don't know what's going to happen, but it feels exciting.'

Indeed, landing the plum job on *Strictly* was more exciting than she could have imagined and thrust her into a whole new spotlight as a television personality. It also placed her one step closer to *The Alesha Show*, that centre-stage TV slot that she often dreamed about.

But as the latest chapter of her life opens, Alesha may have had reservations as she found herself, for the first time, facing some opposition, through no fault of her own. Needless to say, the feisty streak that kept her going through a difficult childhood, her climb to the top of the pop tree, Harvey's affair and her record company's betrayal would carry her through any flack that *Strictly* fans might throw at her. And the same passion, energy and enthusiasm that made her pick herself up from rock bottom and crawl back to the top is bound to win the doubters over after a while.

'I've been through quite a lot and it's always harder when everything is played out in front of the world's media,' the sassy singer has said. 'But I feel happier than ever right now. Everything in life happens for a reason. When I was going through that hard time I picked myself up, dusted myself off and went and won *Strictly*. I like to think I have a fighting spirit.'

The fact that she is returning to the very show that helped her turn her life around means that she will be surrounded by people who love and respect her and understand what she went through to get back up on her dancing feet after being knocked down.

On his chat show in May, Justin Lee Collins asked Alesha whether the show had changed her life. 'Absolutely,' she replied without hesitation. 'It wasn't until the winner was announced and the dust had settled that I actually realized what I had done. Because I had been in a bit of a bubble.

'I was overwhelmed by the public support. That was incredible. It was bigger than I ever imagined. I had a strange feeling at the end of that show that everything was going to be okay. It was a lovely feeling. I was a broken woman at the end, though. My body was covered in bruises. I could hardly walk. But it was worth all the pain.'

As the familiar theme tune rang through the BBC's Studio One on 18 September 2009, a determined Alesha knew she was facing one of her toughest challenges yet. Pulling off an amazing win in *Strictly* and climbing Kilimanjaro for charity had been demanding and exhausting, but had equally served to endear her to the hearts of the nation. Taking over from Arlene in the midst of an ageism row had the potential to turn her new fans against her. It was a big gamble but, according to series seven contestant Phil Tufnell, she took it in her stride.

'Everyone needs time to warm up,' he told the *People* after the first show. 'Alesha wasn't nervous for her first night. She looked great and seemed to be on the ball. I don't think she'll be too nice, and if she judges like she dances, then it's going to be hot.' He also thought her position as an ex-*Strictly* dancer

211

gave Alesha great insight. 'Alesha knows what we go through,' he added.

Before the show, Alesha admitted that she had her doubts about taking on the new role.

'I thought hard about taking the *Strictly* job because, first and foremost, I'm a musician,' she told *The Sun*'s Colin Robertson. 'But I thought this was something I would love to do. I'll just have to multi-task.' And she was shocked at the news that Arlene was out of the show. 'I was surprised that I was replacing Arlene, along with everybody else,' she continued. 'But I understand the industry. Change is important and my feeling is that even if I had said no to the job, a change would have happened. If you're making *Strictly*, you're going to want new features, new formats, new professional dancers – even a new judge. It makes sense to me. I do the same thing when I'm thinking about my music. I think, "Right, what am I going to do differently?" If I didn't, my fans would get bored.

'I don't see my joining *Strictly* as being that deep and, although it's been made into this big debate, the reality is it's still Saturday night entertainment. That's what I'm keeping my focus on ... And I'm not sure about this idea that I've been brought in to attract younger viewers. When I was a contestant on the show, I got fan mail from four-year-olds, thirteen-year-olds, even eighty-two-year-olds.'

With Arlene now commenting on the dances, and the judges, on *The One Show*, the new panel member confessed she had not spoken to her predecessor since signing on the dotted line. 'I haven't spoken to her, but part of me thinks, "That was probably hard. I hope she's OK." I have compassion,' she revealed. 'But I'm a great believer that when one door closes, another opens. And more doors have opened for Arlene so I can only be happy for her now ... I admire her because I think she's had a fantastic career and is a strong woman in the industry. I hope I can have a career that lasts as long.'

One of Alesha's main concerns was upsetting the apple cart where the other three judges were concerned. As close friends of Arlene, she felt they may take against her and make her unwelcome. She was relieved to find her fears were unfounded.

'Arlene was friends with her fellow judges and they were sad to see her go,' she said in *The Sun* interview. 'I didn't want to upset a happy home. So the first time I walked in, I was thinking to myself, "How are they going to be?" It was like I was the new kid at school. They could have been a bit funny with me but they haven't. They've made me feel excited to be there and only ever treated me with respect.'

On the night, Bruce glossed over the controversy joking, 'Some of you may have heard that we have a new judge this year. Alesha, can I welcome you to the show.'

Asked how she felt, Alesha replied, 'I've got the best seat in the house and I'd rather be sitting here because I know exactly how they feel.'

The judges themselves welcomed her with Len jesting, 'I'm very happy that I'm not sitting next to Bruno.'

'Would I rather be sitting next to that ...' Bruno fired back, pointing at Len and then cuddling his new co-judge, '... or this?'

On day one, week one, Alesha's comments were general, and she avoided being too specific on the technical side of the dances. Congratulating Rav Wilding for being the first out she told him he was 'stompy'; she agreed with Len that Ricky Groves' shoulders needed to be raised and told athlete Jade

Johnson and Ian Waite, 'you two look great together.' She was brave enough to disagree with Bruno when he said Chris Hollings looked like he was 'sucking a lemon', and bizarrely commented to Joe Calzaghe, after his dance with Kristina Rihanoff, 'I caught you smelling her hair. You looked like you were smelling her hair at one point.'

In the second show, the following day, Alesha appeared to be getting into her stride. After Jade and Ian's opening cha-cha she commented, 'Cha-cha is one of my favourite dances and this suits you. Personality in abundance. You did a great job.'

She also got her first taste of the frequent rows between judges. After telling Ali Bastian, 'You're simply stunning to watch. One of the most beautiful dancers I've ever seen,' she pretended to chat giggle with Bruno as Len and Craig had a spat over 'posing and posturing' in the rumba.

Ricky Groves' cha-cha had her laughing throughout, but there was a slightly stunned moment when Alesha passed her judgement, saying, 'The most entertaining dance of the night. And he's wearing pink ... he should get points for wearing pink.'

A dance-off between Rav Wilding and Martina Hingis meant Alesha's first taste of the dance-off was a tricky one, and it split the judges in half. While Craig and Alesha chose Martina, Bruno and Len opted to save Rav, and the tennis ace was out.

The first week was over and Alesha could breathe a sigh of relief.

The reaction to her first outing as judge, however, was mixed. The BBC's official website was flooded with polarized opinions from over 2,000 fans. Some were furious at her 'totally pointless' comments, saying she was 'not qualified or experienced enough' and that 'someone should fetch her coat for her now'. One commented, 'I feel sorry for Aleesha [sic], she is a bubbly and likeable performer, but she has been ill-advised in taking on this position.' Others backed her saying, 'Just give the girl a chance. After all, it was not her who asked Arlene to leave.' One post on the message board called her 'superb', and added, 'What *Strictly* has lacked in the past is someone like Alesha; she understands what it is like to be in the non-dancer's shoes and is both constructive and supportive to the non-dancers.'

Judge Craig Revel Horwood jumped to Alesha's defence and asked fans to leave her alone. 'It makes me angry and concerned that people are having a go at her,' he said on *BBC Breakfast News*. 'Give her a chance, for God's sake!'

The BBC also issued a statement backing their new signing. 'We're pleased at how fantastically well Alesha was received for her debut on *Strictly Come Dancing* and delighted that so many people tuned in and enjoyed the show.'

In characteristic style, Alesha brushed off the criticism and refused to let it get her down. 'You can't please all of the people all of the time,' she told the *Daily Mirror*. 'I am not a quitter. It's not in my nature to consider quitting.'

For *Strictly Come Dancing* viewers the warmth, charm and humour which enthralled them during her dancing days is becoming as familiar on the judging panel as Bruno's outrageous similes, Craig's acerbic comments and Len's 'Seven'. And, as ever, her comments are punctuated with the inimitable, gravelly laugh. 'My laugh is filthy,' she confesses. 'I'd change it if I could but it's become a trademark.'

But her new TV career won't prevent her from concentrating on her music career. By August, with *The Alesha Show* now a platinum-selling success, she was already planning her next single, 'Black Cloud', written and produced by N.E.R.D star Chad Hugo. And she was already back in the studio, working on songs for the new album with Kilimanjaro colleague Gary Barlow.

'It makes a change from climbing a mountain for Comic Relief,' she admitted. 'He is so talented – hopefully the songs will be better than the ones we sang round the campfire on Kilimanjaro.'

And, as she prepared for her sellout tour, she insisted that her musical career was not something she was going to give up easily. 'This is a long-term thing,' she told *OK!* magazine. '"The Boy Does Nothing" was a great way to kick off, but some people might have thought it was a novelty record, so it's my job as an artist to prove this is a serious long-term project. I want people to hear the music and relate to it on an emotional level as well.'

Her thirties may also see her achieve another ambition – finding love and settling down. Alesha's newfound happiness means she is ready for romance in the near future and her past knocks are not about to put her off. 'I was taught not to tar people with the same brush,' she says. 'When you come out of a long-term relationship it's about dealing with it, healing, and getting yourself in a nice place so when you meet someone new you're starting afresh. You trust someone until they give you reason not to. It's taken two years but I'm now in the best place I've been in my life.'

Afterword

Looking back over the ten years that had dragged her from heaven to hell and back again, Alesha admitted that life had often been challenging, but the challenge was exactly what she thrived on. 'Everything has an equal part to play,' she said. 'The days of Mis-Teeq were so much fun and that was the beginning of everything for me. And obviously doing *Strictly Come Dancing* was life-changing. Then Kilimanjaro was obviously a great challenge to do. I constantly keep trying to challenge myself with new things. The only way to get better at anything in life is to just put yourself into a risky situation with things that scare you. That's the way to grow as a person and gain more skills in life.'

From a poverty-stricken upbringing in Welwyn Garden City to pop diva, ballroom queen and 'national treasure', Alesha has been through more ups and downs than the average fairground attraction, and right now she's riding high. But without the lows, the chances are she wouldn't be enjoying the view from the top once more.

'I wouldn't change the rollercoaster, not for a second,' she insists. 'I felt it was important to have that moment because it was a good life lesson to never give up and continue working hard.'

The fact that she has been through so much has not only endeared her to the nation but has left her a wiser, more philosophical soul. While the future looks brighter than ever for Alesha, she is not likely to forget her past in a hurry.

'You shouldn't tell people to cheer up when they're sad,' she advises. 'I'm a happy person, but I know that if you're down you have to go through it to come out the other end.'

As someone who has done just that, Alesha remains an inspiration to women everywhere.

Index

Jamelia 90
James, Duncan 200
Jay Z 63, 68
John, Elton 47, 50
Johnson, Jade 213–14
Jones, Gethin 103, 110, 110, 114,
    119, 122, 123, 124, 125
Jones, Tom 50
Judd, Su 107

Keating, Ronan 175, 179–80, 181,
    182, 185
Kilimanjaro 12, 175–89, 216, 217
Kingston, Alex 98
Knight, Beverley 90
Kopylova, Lilia 109

La Scala 39
Lamont, Max 'Jam' 30
Lancaster-Stewart, Penny 103, 104,
    107, 110
Littlewood, Dominic 103
LL Cool J 52
Logan, Gabby, 103, 107
Logan, Kenny, 103
Look But Don't Touch 143–4, 146, 199
Loose Women, 161
Lopez, Jennifer 45
Loughborough University 23
Lucker, Zoe 208
Lytton, Louisa 105, 204

McCartney, Paul 50
McMahon, John, 56
McNally, Zena, 30–1
Madonna 18, 190, 193
Maffia, Lisa 40, 84
Malignaggi, Paulie 175
Marsh, Kym 56
Martin, Ricky 50
Match, The 78, 86
Matthews, Liz 139

Maxim Woman of the Year Awards 51
May, Brian 50
MC Harvey, 11, 32–3, 36, 41–4,
    52–3, 54, 55, 61, 69, 73–4,
    77–9, 82–7, 90, 92–3, 115,
    142, 154, 155, 173–4, 175
MC Neutrino 41
  see also Oxide & Neutrino
MC Romeo 40, 84
MC Shystie 88–9
Mean Fiddler 28
Mercury Records 30
Milestones 98, 196
Ministry of Sound 26, 147
Minogue, Kylie 45, 173
Mis-Teeq 11, 22, 26–40, 46–9, 50–
    3, 54–77, 103, 108, 163, 192
  in America 72–4, 75–7
  Artist of the Year 34
  Cancer Research supported by
    67–8
  Capital FM award for 51
  Destiny's Child compared to 12,
    37–8, 45, 58, 59
  first full UK tour of 63–8
  first live London gig of 38–9
  greatest-hits album of 79–80 (*see
    also* songs and albums)
  in Japan 71
  Maxim award for 51
  MOBO award for 53, 59
  product endorsement by 68
  Queen's Golden Jubilee
    performance of 50
  reunion rumours concerning 149
  selling-out accusation levelled
    against 48
  Shaggy tours with 44, 47
  split 79–81
  spotless reputation of 41
  see also Dixon, Alesha; Nash, Su-
    Elise; Washington, Sabrina